GOD of the Valley

Sean Reed

— Sean Reed —

All rights reserved. No part or this book may be reproduced, copied or transmitted in any form or by any means, electronic or mechanical, including photocopying, recoding or by any informational storage and retrieval system, without permission in writing from the publisher. All references used are cited below.

Library Of Congress

ISBN: 978-1-945454-06-6

Published By: M. Publications LLC

www.MPublications.com

Graphics By: Fletchergraphics

www.Fletchergraphics.com

Copyright ©2018. Sean Reed

Henry T. Mahan writes: '... Christ has removed the substance of death and only a shadow remains. A shadow is there but cannot hurt or destroy.'[6] 4 Henry T. Mahan, With New Testament Eyes, Evangelical Press, vol. i, pp. 18–19.

"Keep your face to the sun and you will never see the shadows." - Helen Keller

[1] Soanes, C., & Stevenson, A. (Eds.). (2004). Concise Oxford English dictionary. Oxford: Oxford University Press.

[2] Soanes, C., & Stevenson, A. (Eds.). (2004). Concise Oxford English dictionary. Oxford: Oxford University Press.

[3] Soanes, C., & Stevenson, A. (Eds.). (2004). Concise Oxford English dictionary. Oxford: Oxford University Press.

[4] Soanes, C., & Stevenson, A. (Eds.). (2004). Concise Oxford English dictionary. Oxford: Oxford University Press.

[5] Soanes, C., & Stevenson, A. (Eds.). (2004). Concise Oxford English dictionary. Oxford: Oxford University Press.

[6] Ellsworth, R. (2006). Opening up Psalms (p. 48). Leominster: Day One Publications.

[1] Tyndale House Publishers. (2013). Holy Bible: New Living Translation (Mt 28:20). Carol Stream, IL: Tyndale House Publishers.

[1] Smith, S., & Cornwall, J. (1998). In The exhaustive dictionary of Bible names. North Brunswick, NJ: Bridge-Logos.

[1] Peterson, E. H. (2005). The Message: the Bible in contemporary language (Je 6:13–14). Colorado Springs, CO: NavPress.

Introduction

> At your greatest point of suffering, in your greatest time of need; by your side you will find Him and forever He will be...The God of the Valley
>
> ~Sean Reed

We will all encounter valleys in our lifetime. It doesn't matter who you are or where you're from or how good or bad you've been; valleys are those moments when life hits us so hard in the gut that the wind gets knocked out of us. A valley is when you walk into the office and they inform you of an unexpected job loss. It's the painful heartbreak of divorce. It may be coping with grief after the loss of a loved one. Not all valleys are created equal; still they share the common thread of discomfort or suffering. Suffering is a common reality of the human experience. Grief will come knocking on all of our doors one day. Life crisis, calamity and failure are inevitable. No one can escape this reality. That's a part of this fallen world that we live in. Yet, even there, in a place of deep anguish and disparity, we can experience hope and victory. In some of the darkest places, we can best appreciate the light. Somehow God uses the fragments from moments that break us into pieces. He can take those fragments and make a masterpiece.

This book is about discovering God in difficult times, how to overcome life's greatest obstacles and getting to know the valley walking God. By the end of our journey you should have a firm grip on the Father's hand. You'll learn how to tap into abundant life in the face of death. It's about being anchored in peace within turbulent storms and acquiring hope amidst what appears to be hopeless situations. If you've ever needed a book to encourage you through a season of darkness, this is it.

In Matthew 28:20 Jesus told His disciples, *"And be sure of this: I am with you always, even to the end of the age."* This is God's promise to His people. The word "always" in the Greek language could also mean "lifetime". The word "end" in Greek could translate as "until completion". So Jesus' statement could read like this: I am present with you through your lifetime, to see it to completion.

Valleys are tough, well, because we can't see Jesus in them. Sometimes we can't feel His presence and at times it seems as if we can't hear His voice. He's with us. We may not understand why we end up in the valley of the shadow of death. But God himself has guaranteed us that Jesus is there to see us through it. He's our Good Shepherd and He will guide us through our lifetime, to our completion.

Throughout the Bible we marvel at the miraculous works of God as He delivered our heroes of faith. But let's think about that for a moment. David faced Goliath and prevailed, but what if there were no giants? Would David have reached the stratosphere of stardom without adversity? Would anyone care about Daniel and the

Hebrew boys with the absence of the fiery furnace, or the den of lions? Abraham and Sarah's inability to have a child or Esther braving death itself as she goes to see the king. What about the Apostle Paul and the crew being shipwrecked but making it to the shore on broken pieces? The list could go on and on.

Throughout these stories we witness the power of God as He enables His people to prevail. We become passengers on their journeys through mountains high and valleys low. We also relate to their pain, their flawed humanity and God's divine redemption. Yet, when it comes to our own stories and walks with God, are we desirous of triumph without first encountering a test?

Your valley may be in the form of sickness, sickness of the soul or in the body. Is it a financial valley? Could it be the valley of a broken heart? This may be a Job season in your life, where your world is falling to pieces. You may be asking yourself, "How do we make it through this? Why hasn't God answered my prayers yet?"

Or, "where is God right now?" As you continue in this book we will strive to answer these questions. For now, consider Psalm 46:1 *(ESV) "God is our refuge and strength, a very present help in trouble."* Help is not only on the way, He is present. He not only sends help, He himself is your help!

Sometimes we're in the valley to learn; sometimes we've made the wrong turn. Either way, God is still there and no matter how harsh the circumstances of life is, our God cares for us deeply. Our Father will make all things work together for our good.

Throughout our journey, you'll discover how to recover hope, joy and peace if you've lost it somewhere along the way. You'll discover nuggets of wisdom within the enriched valley soil. You'll see showers of pain transform into nourishment for your soul.

This book is to equip you to "go through" your current valley or one that you'll encounter in the future.

There will be one in the future. We can't plan the when's and what's of life, but we can prepare for the journey. If you knew that you were going on a cruise in December, you'd prepare for it months prior to that trip. I'm quite sure you'd pack what you need for the cruise. When walking through the valley, there's a preparation of the soul required. Why? So a season of pain doesn't remain. So that you go through the valley and come out on the other side greater than you were going in.

I can't predict when sufferings and trials will happen, but I do know they're coming to us all. When those seasons arrive, we can have a foundation built upon truth. We can be so rooted in God, that when the floods of life rage against us we'll know that we are God's special treasure. That He hasn't abandoned us in the shadows of death. So take this journey with me and discover the God of the Valley.

1. Living in the Shadow of Death

"Keep your face to the sun and you will never see the shadows." -Helen Keller

"Even though I walk through the valley of the shadow of death, I fear no evil, for You are with me"
Psalm 23:4 -King David

Death valley creeps up on us all. One moment you're on top of the mountain in life and everything seems to be flowing smoothly, and then suddenly a darkness creeps in.

One day my family and I were traveling to St. Louis, Mo from Texas. As we were driving through Moore Oklahoma, we saw the massive devastation that was left in the wake of a tornado's utter destruction a few weeks earlier. Everyone paused in amazement as we watched construction crews tirelessly clean up the disastrous rubble. Surprisingly enough, you could see the exact path the tornado had taken by looking to see which buildings were still standing and which ones were crumbled. Wherever the winds of this storm hit, it completely leveled that place.

As our car slowed down to take it all in, my family sat shocked by what we saw. We felt a deeper sense of grief for the families that may have experienced death and loss after that storm. We prayed for the families affected by this tragedy and then silently reflected on the moments we captured while we drove by.

Up to that somber moment, we were enjoying our road trip. I was making good time, and as a bonus the weather was great and it was beautiful day. After passing through Moore though our mood changed, but that wasn't the only thing that changed.

A few miles outside the city the clouds above us shifted from bright and sunny to dark and gloomy. In the wake of the destruction we saw from that tornado, we all had a unified thought of getting away as quickly and safely as possible from the oncoming storm. Rain began to trickle down and then out of nowhere a torrential downpour. It was to the point that we couldn't see our way up ahead. Visibility between each windshield wiper stroke may have just been a few feet ahead. Brake lights from the cars in front of us gave a sense of where the dividing lines of the highway were. We went from cruising speeds of 70mph to a mere walking pace in no time. But did we stop driving? No way! Even if we were at a snails pace, we refused to stay in the potential path of a tornado. We clearly saw what a tornado could do and we knew the impact of its devastation. Many people lost their dreams, hopes were crushed and lives were taken.

My wife decided to pull up the local news report on her I-pad just to tell us that we were in the path of another tornado. The radar showed us that we were right on the edge of the storm. I knew that I could get us out of the pathway if we moved a little faster. So, just as I started to increase my speed, the car began to hydroplane. Moments later while trying not to lose control, lightning sharply struck a highway exit sign literally within 15 feet of us. My children screamed and began to panic. It got worse! Golf-ball sized hail stones of judgment began to fall and smash against the window. The winds picked up so quickly and blew so hard that our car began to sway back and forth as the gusts increased.

I won't lie to you; honestly, I felt absolute fear. I was afraid because I wasn't in control. I was in the valley of the shadow of death. This looked like the end. It was daytime and yet darkness surrounded us and everything that we saw indicated that we should expect the worst. This is what it's like to live in the shadow of death, to be in the presence of immanent danger and feeling helpless with no control to do anything substantial about it. When no matter what, the rain keeps pouring down. And just when you think you've caught a break from the drama. The lightning flashes and the hailstones come flying in from all directions.

"Even though I walk through the valley of the shadow of death, I fear no evil, for You are with me"

Psalm 23:4 -King David

King David, in the 23rd Psalm paints a picture that may parallel your pain. He speaks of an experience that may be your present reality. David calls this place "The Valley of the Shadow of Death". He walks through this place in his life that maybe we can all relate to in some way or another. Just for a moment, let's take a walk with David in the valley.

As we dive into David's poem, lets start by unpacking the definitions of a few terms that we'll use quite frequently throughout this chapter. The first definition is of the word valley. The Concise Oxford English Dictionary defines these as:

Valley: a low area between hills or mountains, typically with a river or stream flowing through it.

Shadow: a dark area or shape produced by a body coming between light rays and a surface.

Death: the personification of the power that destroys life; the destruction or end of something.

Some of you reading this have lost your business. But it was more than income for you...it was your dream. You may have received a negative prognosis from the doctor and you've questioned why has God allowed this to happen. You may have lost your marriage and you are disappointed that things haven't turned out the way you envision by this stage in your life. But whatever you may be facing my dear friend, I want you to know that you are living in a shadow of death. If you would, please repeat that statement in your mind, if you can say it out loud: I am living in a shadow of death. This may not feel like a bombshell revelation, but it's powerful. The truth is, Jesus conquered death through the finished work of the cross. Paul, The Apostle, told us that Jesus took the sting out of death and it is now only a shadow or a former shell of itself.

Please realize that while you are reading this book, you're still alive. Although everything around you may reek of death, **YOU** are still here. You are present in your valley and you still have life! There is also One who is with you and He happens to be The Good Shepherd who can protect you from evil. He will see you through to the other side.

Now, back to our text. David isn't afraid of the evil here because he is secure in the presence of the Lord. Yet, there's evil present in the valley. This conveys to us that walking with God doesn't necessarily negate suffering in our lives.

Becoming a Christian doesn't mean the absence of evil circumstances. God never promises us that we wouldn't face difficulties in this fallen world. In fact, the Bible says in several passages that believers will experience suffering. But also promises us victory through God's power.

> *"Many are the afflictions of the righteous,*
> *but the Lord delivers him out of them all."*
> *Psalm 34:19 (NASB95)*

My family and I were traveling to visit relatives in St. Louis when the storm came. This wasn't God's judgment for something that we had done wrong. This wasn't even God punishment against us. My friend, please receive this right now, God loves you. It's going to be difficult for you to make it through the valley if you believe that God is out to punish you. You do have an adversary in the kingdom of darkness, Satan, who seeks to kill, steal and destroy. But God isn't in Heaven filled with an eagerness to harm his children. There's no hope for help if your image of God isn't healthy. God is our Heavenly

Father and He's your Daddy who loves you and will be with you through the valleys of life. Now, with that being said, just because He loves you doesn't mean that He has to remove affliction or suffering from our lives. A good Father knows that adversity develops character. And without trouble there's no triumph. Without problems how can we prevail? Where there's no test, how do you know if your faith has graduated to the next level?

When a parent is raising an infant, they look forward to that child's development and growth. Part of that growth process includes pain. The benefit of chewing comes with the growth pain of teething. The benefit of walking comes with the growth pain of falling. No matter how much we love an infant, growth pains are inevitable, but they're also beneficial.

You may not understand the benefits of your growing pains yet, but here's what you can count on: God is with you! This statement implies that you and your Heavenly Father are alive. That means whatever shadow of death that's been cast ahead of you, hasn't prospered against you. You have prevailed and you will prevail. As we read a few verses surrounding Ps. 34 we can receive the promises of the Good Shepherds provision.

"The righteous cry, and the Lord hears and delivers them out of all their troubles. The Lord is near to the brokenhearted and saves those who are crushed in spirit. Many are the afflictions of the righteous, but the Lord delivers him out of them all."
Psalm 34:17–19 (NASB95)

Do you feel crushed in your spirit by the betrayal of a loved one or close friend? Is your world falling apart faster than you can patch it back together? Will you cry out to God for help? God will deliver you out of all the afflictions of your soul, but I must warn you, there's a difference between a prayer of faith and a cry of anger. There's a difference between casting a care to God and submitting to Him a complaint. There's a difference between praying in faith and panicking with fear.

As I admitted before, while traveling through the storm that day I felt fear. I was afraid and although I tried to be...I wasn't in control. At the sight of a potential tornado touching down, it had my family and me in a frantic state. But as I began to pray within, I remained calm. I can recall praying something along these lines, "This cannot be the end of my story, there's too much that You have for us to do. You are with us and I receive Your peace in this chaos. God, you are in control even of the storm."

There was a calm that hit me at that moment. It was a peace that literally passed my understanding. Now let me be clear, the weather didn't change outside, but the storm of fear that was brewing inside of me did. When Jesus calmed the storm within me, I wasn't afraid of the storm around me anymore. I knew God would somehow guide me through this and protect my family.

I began to sing a song of worship to the Lord. I can say that I was in the valley of the shadow of death, but

I wasn't afraid for my families well being. God was with us and I know the God of all peace can be your valley walker today if you allow Him to be.

The Truth about Shadows

Remember a shadow is a dark area or shape produced by a body coming between light rays and a surface. And death is the personification of the power that destroys life.

As a kid, we used to turn off the lights in our room and pull out our flashlights. The flashlight would be the only light on in the room and we'd point it at the wall. We would stick our hands in-between the flashlight and the wall making shapes of bunny ears and spiders with our fingers. I'm sure you've played this game before and if you haven't you should try it. Just like making shadows on the wall with flashlights, the adversary makes shadows in the valley.

The source of light is God. Then there's the body that comes between the light rays and the surface. That's the evil one, your adversary. There's a figure on the wall, the personification of your destruction or end of something, death.

Your shape may be different than mine, but we have all seen shapes that can cast a shadow of our destruction. Satan is a master of deception, but he's only a shadow-maker beneath the glory of the life-giver. The shadow is cast by the brilliance of the light behind the object. In other words, there can be no shadow without the light behind it. If there is the presence of evil, it directly implies the existence of good! If there are clouds, there's got to be a sun behind them. If there is darkness, it is not greater than light beyond the momentary overcast.

Yes, there is a shadow in the valley, but you can walk through it fearing no evil. The image of death pales in comparison to the substance of life. Life is eternal and any form of death is temporal. Life comes from the Lifegiver, our Father God, who is eternal by nature. The Eternal One walks with you to supply everlasting victory for the temporary afflictions of your soul. That's why He's able to deliver you out of them all, because He outlasts them all.

Be encouraged my brother and sister, the shadow may be cast but it's not the reality that it appears to be. What I am saying is though you have genuinely experienced storms around you, you can also experience peace in the storm. How can one have hope from hopeless situations and strength even in time of weakness? You have to believe that the reality of life is greater than the reality of death. You have to believe that what we have received in the person of Father God is the actual giver of life. It is only Him who causes things to live and light to come out of darkness. And it is only Him who can make something out of nothing.

You may say that some things have perished in your life and people may respond, "I'm sorry for your loss." I'd like to propose that your God can make dead things live again. He shares with us His eternity and He shares with us eternal victory.

The Power of Life

If death is the destruction or end of something, then what exactly is life? To try and define life let's reflect on Jesus in action when He raised Lazarus from the dead. If we review this scripture, what can we ask ourselves?

John 11:1–14 (NLT)

How did Lazarus become sick? Was he sick because God was punishing him? Is Lazarus sick because he lacks faith? Does God's love for Lazarus run out? If you look at verse 5, it states that Jesus loved them all. This makes it clear to us, that bad things will still happen to good people, even the people whom God loves. Here is a simple but powerful lesson. The litmus test of God's love for us isn't the level of pain, problems or suffering we face in this life. God is love and He cares for you unconditionally.

Lazarus' sickness isn't a punishment or judgment against him. How he becomes ill is irrelevant. The reality is, he is sick. Why, however, is stated in verse 4: *"... So that the Son of God will receive glory."* What does that mean exactly? Let us go back a little in the verse and you will hear Jesus say, *"Lazarus sickness will not end in death."* In other words, death won't have the final say.

Things are not always as they appear to be in your life. What appears to be for your destruction may only be shadows cast in the glorious light of God. He's going to get the glory out of what you are going through. Keep 'you' faith and hope in the Lord! He will raise you up from whatever is weighing you down.

Now, verse 5 says that Jesus loves them, but verse 6 tells us that Jesus stayed where He was. In other words, He didn't go to meet Lazarus to solve the problem immediately. He didn't soothe the pain of those He loved in the timeframe desired.

Have you ever experienced disappointments from God's delays? Lazarus is about to die of a health issue and Jesus doesn't rush to stop death in its tracks. However, at the right time Jesus says, let's go. In your own life, He will do the same. Trust God to deliver you out of all your afflictions, but give Him room to do it in a manner and time that He chooses. You will have to release control of something that you may care about into His hands. And the only way you'll do that is if you realize you are releasing control of your cares to the One who cares for you.

In verse 9 Jesus says,

"During the day people can walk safely. They can see because they have the light of this world. 10 But at night there is danger of stumbling because they have no light."

We love to see where we are going. It gives us security to see God working things out. When it's daytime, we rely on the sun, but the challenge for us is that when we can't see our way in this world, we stumble. In other words, do we rely on the greater light of God to guide us when we can't see our way in this world?"

Lazarus and his family were about to face a dark time. The shadow of death was on them and Jesus was well aware of the tragedy to come. Verse 14 lets us know that Lazarus is dead. Yet, in the next verse, Jesus speaks as if they are about to shake his hand and talk with him: *"Come let's go see him."*

John 11:20–44 (NLT)

If you read verse 20-29, we can simply ask ourselves, how many times have I exhibited this kind of faith? Can you relate to this reaction? Martha's replies to Jesus show that she believed in the resurrection from the dead at a future time. But Jesus was implying that faith in Him at that very moment could cause life to spring forth.

"32 When Mary arrived and saw Jesus, she fell at his feet and said, 'Lord, if only you had been here, my brother would not have died.' 33 When Jesus saw her weeping and saw the other people wailing with her, a deep anger welled up within him, and he was deeply troubled. 34 'Where have you put him?' He asked them."

Wait, why is Jesus angry? Was it due to the people placing the blame of Lazarus' death on Jesus' poor timing? Jesus is being accused of failing His loved ones. He didn't come through for them as they had hoped. They felt abandoned in their valley. They spoke as if death had prevailed, and Jesus wept because of **their** unbelief.

Is this your mindset? Is this how you feel or speak regarding your dreams? Is this how you have expressed your thoughts to someone about your valley right now? Jesus get's angry and goes right to the grave.

I want to ask you, where have you put "him," your dream, your loved one, your purpose, your children, your ministry, your church? Where have you buried it to see it no more? Where have you declared, its over? Where have you said, I'm sorry for my loss...end of sentence, end of book. What have you declared as a defeat to the grip of death? Point Jesus to it and see what He has to say about it:

For some of you, you may have a calling to write books, plays or even produce movies. Many of you have dreams of having a child, but doctors have said it's not possible. For someone, this is your hope of having a healthy marriage. For others, you have lost a loved one and the weight of grief is overwhelming. I don't know where you are right now in your life, but Jesus is available to you. If you invite Him to come and see, He will shine the glory of God into the darkest situations. He will produce life right in the face of death.

Jesus weeps, not because he's helpless but because they were hopeless. They feared death more than they feared life. They believed in the grave as a reality more than they believed in the resurrection. They believed the bad report, but struggled with the report of The Lord. Roll the stone aside and make room for God. Martha says, *"There's a terrible smell if we open up that place of death."* But Jesus said in effect, *"If you believe Me, you will have the power of life to triumph over death!"* Jesus doesn't weep in grief over death. Jesus is the life himself! *"Lazarus, come out!"* This is life in action. One word from God, while walking in the valley of death, can change your life completely.

Let's not anger God by making Him smaller in our hearts than our pain. Let's not doubt God's ability to take the hurt away. Instead, bring Him to the place of our problem and watch Him work His wonders.

The shadow-maker is no match for the Light-giver. Let's make up in our minds to release the offense against

God for what may appear to be abandonment in your time of need. Let's understand that divine providence isn't void of God's compassion. Whatever suffering you face in life, Jesus the Shepherd will step right into it and experience your suffering with you.

God Help Us

"For we do not have a high priest who is unable to empathize with our weaknesses, but we have one who has been tempted in every way, just as we are--yet he did not sin. Let us then approach God's throne of grace with confidence, so that we may receive mercy and find grace to help us in our time of need." Hebrews 4:15–16 (NIV)

Several thoughts race through my head when I consider these verses of scripture amidst the backdrop of the Lazarus story. One thought is this: how would Lazarus, Mary and Martha face this valley if they had to do it all over again? For example sake, having experienced this event, let's say a week passes by and Lazarus comes down with another blow of sickness. Now that they have see death conquered by life, good swallow up evil, healing triumphant over sickness...how would they handle it?

Would they be upset if Jesus took His time again? Would they call for the mourners to follow them around weeping? Would their understanding of death as the end change? Now that they have seen the corpse that "stinketh" in grave clothes newly recycled for life again, how would they react? I believe their fears would subside and death wouldn't have the same ring of finality to it. Sickness wouldn't feel good, but sickness wouldn't be the end either. Instead of them blaming God for their loss, I think they would simply say again, come see where Lazarus lay. They would approach Jesus, not as a mere man limited by space and time, but they would see the throne of grace. They would approach Him with confidence that they'd receive mercy and find grace to help them in their time of need. They would understand that Jesus feels their pain and could heal their pain.

Lazarus' name is significant. Names had meanings in the Bible days, as with our names today. Lazarus is a Greek translation of the name Eleazar. Eleazar means: God has helped. God has helped us in the past, He will help us in our present and He will help us in our future. God wants to do it. He is right there with you in the valley. You may not be able to see Him and at times you may not even feel Him, but I ask you to remember the times that God had answered your prayers. I mean, write down the prayers that you've prayed where God replied... *"Jot this down."* Remember those moments where the Lord delivered you out in times past. Satan would love for you to forget what God has done for you in your life. He would love for nothing more than to cast a shadow of doubt on you so great that you forget to fall back on the same chest of your Heavenly Father. He would love for you to forget how the Holy Spirit comforted you before this moment. God has helped you and me and He is willing to help us again.

Though you walk through the valley of the shadow of death, you also walk in the actual presence of life. You walk with the good shepherd. Hear the words of Jesus:

"I am the good shepherd. The good shepherd gives his life for the sheep." (John 10:11).

He offers HIS LIFE for His sheep. He gives life and light to us. Take that life to the place where destruction lay. Allow God to resurrect your dreams and your life.

If you have lost a loved one and they have died in the Lord, please rejoice in the fact that you will see them again. They are in the presence of The Lord as we speak.

"For we walk by faith, not by sight-- we are of good courage, I say, and prefer rather to be absent from the body and to be at home with the Lord." 2 Corinthians 5:7–8 (NASB95)

Death is merely a shadow cast from the reality of presence of life. Shouldn't life receive the greater reverence? Shouldn't life then be glorified and praised rather than death? Shouldn't we rejoice in victory rather than cower in defeat?

2. Shepherd of The Valley

"If there is no struggle, there is no progress...
Power concedes nothing without a demand.
It never did and it never will."
~Frederick Douglass

"The Lord is my shepherd, I shall not want. He makes me lie down in green pastures; He leads me beside quiet waters. He restores my soul; He guides me in the paths of righteousness for His name's sake. Even though I walk through the valley of the shadow of death, I fear no evil, for You are with me; Your rod and Your staff, they comfort me."
Psalm 23:1–4 (NASB95)

This may be one of the most famous passages of scripture in the Bible. King David wrote this Psalm, which is a poem or a song to God. He used a metaphor of our Heavenly Father as a Shepherd, which is fitting to David. David was a shepherd to a flock of sheep he tended as a young man. As David considered how he had to protect, guide and feed his sheep through valleys, streams and grasslands; he wrote to The Lord a song of praise. As we read this song of praise in English, we may miss a few important nuggets of truth that I'd like to bring to the surface.

David said, *"The Lord is my Shepherd"* and because of this, I will not lack. The title "The Lord" in Hebrew is actually a name for God. Yahweh. This is the personal name of God. Sometimes when we simply see "The Lord," the deep meaning of His name gets lost in translation. So what's the significance to God's personal name, Yahweh?

Yahweh: in Hebrew: "The Lord"

Well, this is God's covenant name signifying the living presence of God dwelling with us. He is Yahweh, the ever-present God. The name translated as a verb in Aramaic is: To Be. In other words, The Shepherd for his sheep exists to be what we need. He will be our provision and provider. If we're lost and trapped on every side, He's our way-maker. When we're exposed to the harsh realities of life, He is our shelter.

The Lord: in Aramaic: "To Be"

Jehovah is the Eternal covenant keeping God who always is. The, I AM THAT I AM. He was, is and will be the LORD God. This name reveals God, as the One Who is absolutely self-existent. Who, in Himself possesses essential life and permanent existence. Jehovah comes from the Hebrew verb *"havah,"* which means to exist. He has no beginning and no end. He is and always will be. No matter what we face it can't outlast our everlasting supply. No matter how bad it gets, it won't outlast God's goodness. He exists to give you a full life in the valley of the shadow of death. In Him there's a reservoir of joy, peace, righteousness, love, patience, kindness and long-suffering. He provides for both our spiritual and physical needs. God is our inexhaustible and eternal source. There's no end to His supply. The Lord is! He exist "To Be" our eternal supply. Build your confident expectation on this truth. He's your Shepherd, your eternal source.

Now connect that name with the title of Shepherd. What does a shepherd do? They care for the needs of the flock. The flock has to eat, so it's his responsibility to lead them. He leads them to a feeding ground. He finds grass for feeding and 'need' meeting.

Yahweh exists to be your Shepherd in this life and the life to come. He will provide what you need. Paul encouraged the Church at Philippi:

"And this same God who takes care of me will supply all your needs from his glorious riches, which have been given to us in Christ Jesus."
Philippians 4:19 (NLT)

There's no need to worry about your life. In fact, you can't gain anything by worrying about life. Rather than expending energy on stress, fear and worry, invest your time in worship. Confess as David did that Yahweh is Shepherd who supplies all of your needs.

Have you ever watched an infomercial and they explain the benefits of their product? You know what comes next: "but wait there's more." Today, I have the privilege of saying to you, "but wait there's more." Not only do Shepherds provide for their sheep but they protect sheep from danger as well. Why? I'll tell you, because He cares for them. No different than how dog or cat lovers would risk their life to save their pet. A good shepherd would give his life for their sheep. Jesus is that kind of Shepherd.

This is of course a figurative expression. Don't worry; I'm not saying you're an animal. David's beautiful metaphor helps us to envision His ability to protect us from harm. Yet, this doesn't mean that life is pain free. It doesn't exclude struggles, but it does guarantee that God keeps us. What do I mean by that? I mean He will keep your spirit and soul intact. For instance, money will come and sometimes it'll go, but you will have what you need because The Shepherd will keep you. Sometimes friends will come and other times they'll leave you, but you'll never be alone. You're not a looser because of your losses. God will protect your heart and peace of mind if you let Him.

I want to encourage you to get close to The Shepherd through difficult moments when your faith is being tested. How do you remain close to Him? Spend quality time with Him in prayer. Throughout your day worship and praise God for all that He is and what He's done for you. Also, fellowship with other faith-filled believers and seek out godly-counsel in a time of despair. Recite God's promises over your life and meditate on His truth. Sing spiritual songs as you're going through your day. Make time to tune out the noise so you can listen to the Holy Spirit. These are ways to get close to God in the time of testing.

Now, there's another word in that first verse of Psalms 23 that leads to the good part, *"I shall not want."* We've discussed The Lord as Shepherd, but there's a word that's significant within the verse. The Lord is My Shepherd, so I lack nothing.

The Lord can be your personal provider and guide. He can speak to you and lead you to what's best for you. He can speak to you and provide peace within you in a season of chaos. He is within you so that you shall not want for another hit of a drug, because He takes you higher than any narcotic. He is within you to relax your emotions when someone has betrayed you or your loved ones. He's there to release within you His personal patience when you feel that you can't hold out another moment. But you must trust Him to be your Shepherd. Then call on Him by faith! Faith-filled prayers grant us access to the Lord's divine provision. In His presence you'll find contentment for your soul.

Your faith has to declare that He is available to you. Your faith has to be strong in God as your personal salvation. That He's an active participant in your life right now at this moment. Here's an example of this in action. Take the afore mentioned scripture from Apostle Paul:

"And this same God who takes care of me will supply all your needs from his glorious riches, which have been given to us in Christ Jesus." Philippians 4:19 (NLT)

This is Paul declaring to the people what he believed God was capable of doing, but you've got to receive that in your heart. Lay hold to that truth and make it personal by declaring it over your life. *"Heavenly Father, you will take care of me. And at this moment from your glorious riches in Christ Jesus my Shepherd, all my needs are supplied. I have nothing to worry about or to fear."* Now that sounds like what David said! The Lord is my Shepherd, I shall not...want.

I don't know what you think you lack, but as long as God is in control, there should be a "shall not" in some area. I shall not lust for that because God has supplied my needs. I shall not covet that because what God has for me is for me. I shall not be bitter because I have the power to forgive. I shall not complain because I'm too busy praising God for His many benefits.

It's Getting Hot in Here

Let's head to the book of Daniel in the Old Testament of the Bible to examine an amazing story of deliverance. We are diving into the story after King Nebuchadnezzar of the Babylonian empire made a decree. This law or decree stated that everyone including the Jewish people had to bow down and worship Nebuchadnezzar's statue at the sound of music and instruments. Daniel, Shadrach, Meshach, and Abednego refused to bow down and worship, as this would be idolatry. They worshiped the Lord only. You can follow along and read this story in Daniel 3: 9-28.

If you've ever wondered what faith looks like, this is faith at its best! They believed that God was capable of delivering them from the flames of death. But even if He didn't, God was the only one who would receive praise and honor from their lives. They would trust Him through the furnace of affliction. Their lives were in God's hands no matter what. They had the kind of faith that knew God's power was greater than the illusion of power their adversary appeared to have over them. As you believe like this despite the disadvantages set before your eyes, you make room for God to be gloried! You make room for God to show up and show out. If you continue to read the story, Daniel 3: 19-28, you'll see Nebuchadnezzar ends up worshipping their God. He had to give glory to the true King all because these boys were willing to walk by faith in the face of their adversity. The world needs to see Jesus show up in the flames of affliction. Jesus will dance with you in the fires meant to kill you! When it appears that you're on your own going into the flames. There's only One walking with you who can preserve you, even though the flame is turned up seven times hotter.

Some of you turned up your faith and when you did the problems intensified! Don't back down now, Jesus will keep you from what was designed to kill you! He's your Shepherd who walked with you into the furnace. These believers actually walk out of the furnace of affliction!

Yes, though you walk "through" the valley of the shadow of death, remember He's with you. Yahweh makes all the difference. You may not have the material things that you think you need to make it, but Jesus is more than enough! He is your personal Provider with a never-ending supply.

Don't allow your oppressor to become the god that you worship. Don't offer the worship of fear to your terrorizer. Don't offer praises of worry to your problem.

Refuse to bow at the blast of your enemy. He plays a tune in your ear and he expects you to bow and sing a sad song of "woe is me," but not this time, you'll sing a song of faith in your God.

If you've lost a loved one in your life and holidays are tough to endure. Shed your tears of sadness knowing you won't see them for a while, but then reflect on the good times and rejoice that you'll see them again. Turn birthdays or holidays into a healthy season of reflection and rejoicing.

There's healthy grieving and then there's depression, denial and disconnection. If you've found yourself in a pit of despair I encourage you to seek grief counseling. The Good Shepherd walks with us through Death Valley and sometimes He helps you through other people. If you're struggling in this area find a grief recovery group today. Get the healing you need to live your life in freedom.

You're still alive! There's a life for you to live and purpose for you to fulfill. I'm praying for you. I pray that you will understand there's a time to weep and then there's a time to rejoice. Refuse to bow down to depression. Realize that it's your time to live again!

Make the effort to seek out grief counseling at your local church or research resources in your community, but isolation is not the best option. You know, when the Hebrew boys went into the furnace...at least they had someone to go in there with them. The Lord is a Shepherd to a flock. A flock is a gathering of sheep. Isn't it interesting how in times of grief or hurt we fall into isolation and darkness? We don't want to talk or hang around groups of people. It's like a "shadow of death and depression." But there's healing in the flock! There's victory in the family of faith. Find healthy believers and go to where they are! Worship with them. Fight back against that spirit of depression that seeks to overtake you. Know that God is with you even in the flames of grief as He was with Daniel, the Hebrew boys, Mary, Martha and Lazarus.

At this moment, claim your God-given right to approach The Shepherd of your soul. Receive from Him grace and mercy. Worship Him and receive His love for you. Accept His divine provision over your life. Claim Him as your Shepherd and declare that you shall not want.

"So be truly glad. There is wonderful joy ahead, even though you have to endure many trials for a little while. These trials will show that your faith is genuine. It is being tested as fire tests and purifies gold--though your faith is far more precious than mere gold. So when your faith remains strong through many trials, it will bring you much praise and glory and honor on the day when Jesus Christ is revealed to the whole world."
1 Peter 1:6–7 (NLT)

Fight the Good Fight of Faith

Over the last 4 years of my life I've won a lifelong struggle with weight loss. For much of my life I was overweight. I'm grateful that I can now say that I'm healthy and winning the battle of the bulge. Though the journey has been rewarding, it has also been a daily struggle. Every step on the treadmill was like spiritual warfare! Resisting every cake that was calling me by name felt like trench warfare and every day the pillow arrested me and prevailed over my will to feel the pain of exercise. That struggle was real! Yet, I am grateful for the struggle now that I've come to the other side.

The hardest part for me at the gym was seeing those individuals who were on the physically fit side. You know, those individuals who appeared to love health and fitness. Folks who sort of smiled at 5:30am upon entering the thunder-dome of bodybuilding. I was so far from being ripped and toned. Years away from my goals and dreams of being healthy and in shape, but I also hated being in the condition that I was in.

One day something snapped within me. I stopped envying and coveting their bodies and started to focus on my own future. I began celebrating small daily victories. My current pain would lead to my future gain. The process of attaining health was all a test and I determined within myself to pass it. Some tests of life are tests of our faith. If you persevere through the pain it will produce a healthier stronger version of you.

Peter puts to pen words that ring with The Truth, but honestly, it didn't stir my enthusiasm. No more than my enthusiasm to get out of the bed and get to the gym on a cold winters morning. No more than my enthusiasm to pass up on another deep-fried morsel of goodness to my tongue. Peter is stating that enduring a faith-struggle has advantages. One of which is revealing to us and the people around you, whether your faith is genuinely in God or not.

He goes so far with this thought in verse 6 that he says to be glad, because there's joy ahead. Why? Because our troubles are only for a little while. Faith says, you believe your loving Heavenly Father is with you right now.

It say's, He is present with you in every moment of your life and no matter what life has thrown at you, you have victory over it.

Peter encourages us to endure "it" by faith. I don't know what your "it" is, but you can outlast this moment of testing. God will see to it, personally! He **will** strengthen you and He won't fail you! God will right the wrongs that have occurred in your life. He will grant justice for the crimes committed against you. The Father will restore all that's been stolen from you. Peter says, when Jesus shows up before the whole world, it will have all been worth it. To cleave to your faith in God, despite the fact that your world maybe shattered all around you, Jesus is within you and He will strengthen you, as you trust in Him.

3. There's No God in The Valley

Faith is taking the first step even when you don't see the whole staircase. - Martin Luther King, Jr.

Faith is confidence in God's ability and willingness to keep His promises. It's trusting our Heavenly Father to do what He promised He'd do. When you're walking in faith you're not wishing. You know that God is able and willing to do what He said He would do. The Bible tells us that righteous people live by faith. So you and I should make a habit of trusting in God. Faith in action would look something like this. Let's take the promise of salvation found in *Romans 10:9-10.*

"Because, if you confess with your mouth that Jesus is Lord and believe in your heart that God raised him from the dead, you will be saved. For with the heart one believes and is justified, and with the mouth one confesses and is saved."
Romans 10:9–10 (ESV)

"If you believe in your heart and confess with your mouth..."
Romans 10:8-9

Heart trust leads to a confession of a confident hope. You believe and therefore you speak. Having made this confession of faith, something changed. You weren't saved from sin and death before that confession. Had you died before accepting God's promise of salvation by faith through His grace, you were condemned to Hell. The power of faith in the promise of God in this case has eternal ramifications.

As a result, you'll be with God for all eternity. I'd say salvation is a great deal. You get a relationship with God, filled with His Spirit and you receive a new identity in Christ. You're forever changed in a moment of sincere faith in a biblical promise. You're accepting God's promises as your reality. You then act upon that new truth.

Now, you may not feel like you're going to Heaven, but do you believe that Heaven is real? It may seem like Hell is a fairytale, but are you glad you're not going? If you died today are you confident that you'd leave the body and be present with The Lord? Do you believe today that all of your sins are washed away?

These are the fundamental benefits of salvation. Yet for all those benefits, you can't see God, Heaven, grace or forgiveness. Still a person walking by faith believes that something has changed within their eternal status. That person believes right now, they are saved by faith through God's grace. No one can talk them out of it! It's real no matter how they feel. They're confident in God's ability and willingness to keep His promise for salvation. Believers reading this book would agree with this perspective. You believe God and His promise of salvation and as a proof of this truth, The Holy Spirit bears witness of this reality in our hearts.

The Seesaw of Belief

Now maybe you truly believe God for Heaven, but have you found yourself doubting God in another area of life? Ever second-guess His trustworthiness over the temporal? Maybe not for the big celestial things but for the little earthly things. Or maybe you could be the opposite, you trust God for the small, but not for all of it.

We can be confident in God's willingness to fulfill a promise in one area of our lives and doubt Him in another. It may be that you've prayed and not received a reply in the timeframe you gave God. Did that shake your confidence in prayer? Does prayer work for all areas? Or, does God only do miracles for some people but not others? If so, what gets one prayer through and why does it seem that some prayers go unanswered?

I've found myself angry with God at times because it seemed like He was ignoring my cry for help. Times of suffering, confusion, or disappointment left me open to questioning God. Is He hearing me now? If not, what did I do wrong to cause Him to ignore me?

Why does it seem like He came through for someone over there, but I'm struggling to make it by over here? How is it that the evildoers seem to be doing well, but I'm getting the worst of luck? These thoughts dominated my heart and mind.

You probably had bouts with doubt as well. It wasn't until I walked through a few valleys that I realized what was going on. I had great faith on the mountaintop where everything was bright and sunny, when life was going great. I even had strong faith when I was halfway up the mountain; it wasn't all good, but not all so bad either.

It was my low faith that was the problem; trusting in God's willingness and ability to keep His promises in the face of my greatest problems held me back. Do you feel this way when life seems uncertain? When pain is at its most intense? When prayers take longer to get answered?

In these moments it's like He's the God of the mountain, but not the *God of the Valley*. He can get us into Heaven later on, but for now we've got to endure Hell on earth. To help us rise on the right side of this seesaw of faith and doubt, there's a great story in the Bible about a guy named Ben-hadad. His story will help us learn a valuable lesson. He led about 100,000 Syrian warriors against The Israelites.

If you follow along in *1Kings 20: 26-30,* you will see in this story, and in all fairness to the Syrians, they didn't completely doubt God's existence. They couldn't deny Him because they'd seen Jehovah perform miracles in previous battles. There was no way this small nation could amass big victories in war except through supernatural intervention. You and I can say the same. If it had not been for The Lord on our side, where would we be? Now consider this, it is one thing for you to acknowledge this, but its another for your enemies to say that for you!

Ben-hadad went to Aphek against Israel nonetheless and it appeared to be a strategic opportunity. He'd heard about God's awesome power on the mountain ranges, but he had never heard of God giving Israel victory in the valley. In doing so, the Syrians denied His omnipresence. As if there was a barrier blocking His omniscience and omnipotence on the way down the mountain.

Unfortunately, I've insulted God in a similar manner throughout my life; questioning His willingness to provide and protect. Sometimes the degree of suffering allowed against me warped my perspective of God in the valley. After the afflictions I've endured and seeing what I've seen others suffer through, my faith wavered. When we see massive amounts of pain, sickness, oppression or hopelessness it can take a toll on our faith. It's not that we deny God's existence, but we may question why He allows it. What takes Him so long to bring vengeance, to right the wrongs and or to fix the broken things?

As I peered into the horror of suffering in the valley, the beauty of God's love on the mountain began to dissipate in my mind. Have you ever found yourself shift from faith to doubt like waves of the ocean? A strong tide of faith at one moment rushing in at morning prayer gets brushed back by a series of unfortunate events throughout the day.

What's happening to us is a mind game. It's war over belief. It is not a doubting of God's existence, but in His character. Will He provide as a parent? Does He care for His children? Can He deliver us from this destruction? Do you think that He's the God that can save you but not keep you? The One who carried the cross at Calvary but won't hold your hand through surgery? The One who provided the Lamb to pay my ransom, won't provide a job to pay my bills? He can come and live in my heart but can't heal it when it's broken. You may have faith that God can forgive, but He hasn't forgiven it all. You have the faith that God can forgive you from Heaven but you can't forgive someone who's hurt you on earth.

Is He Only God on the Mountain?

The Mountains in the Bible figuratively represent the high places. To doubt victory in the valley says that He rules the cosmos but doesn't get involved in the common affairs on earth. He's great with the heavenly celestial things, but not the everyday earthly struggles.

Please, don't make the mistake that Ben-hadad made. Jesus is seated in Heaven, but don't forget that He lived as a man on earth as well. He is touched by our infirmities and God is the Creator of both the heavens and the earth. Heaven is His throne and the earth His footstool. There's no place that's too high or too low for Him to reach. We should possess the same confidence on the mountain as we do in the lowest valley. We walk by faith and not by sight or physical senses.

During that battle, both Syrian and Jew stood in awe. The flock of kids became an army of warriors. As Gods flock of sheep, He converts the wimpy into warriors. The great One lives in you and He's greater than the opposition around you.

A human being can have a desire to walk in faith, but also a habit of living in doubt. We may find ourselves embracing a double-minded culture. We must fight this fight of faith and eradicate all doubt! This phrase "double-minded" means: to be facing and trying to go in two opposing directions at the same time. So, trying to walk in faith and doubt at the same time will tear you apart. It's impossible to do. It's like saying I'm praying but I don't know if anything will change. God is real, but if He loved me why would He allow this?

I don't believe God causes suffering in this world, but can He use it to teach, strengthen and build us up? Absolutely. We may not always understand in the temporal the value of a difficult situation, but I do believe we can trust God's purpose of all things. He has a Master plan and nothing will stop Him from seeing your life complete its destiny.

There's no place that our enemy can strategically gain an advantage over us, or God for that matter. So, whether on the mountaintop or the valley, know that there is no limit to Gods reach. He's not only God of the mountains, but He's also *God of the Valley*.

Lessons from Low Times

There are so many wonderful days in our journey of life. I'm sure you've experienced a euphoric sunset that took your breath away. What about those days when everything just felt right with the world? Jokes were funnier, traffic was a breeze and you accomplished something amazing. These are the days that we would love to have, well, everyday.

The reality of life, however, simply put, is marvelously complex. On one side of the city there's the birth of a first child and it'll be a day that family will never forget. While on the other side of town, there's the unexpected passing of a loved one. Sadly, a day the family will also never forget. Someone's getting married and there's dancing and rejoicing as two world merge into one. While another couple sits in divorce court filled with grief as their home falls apart. Some say you have to take the good with the bad. Or, that life wont always be sunny and there are high times and low times. I think we all know this, but it still doesn't make your low seasons any easier to stomach. I want to speak to someone in this chapter about rising above the lows.

If you haven't had that day hit you yet, keep living. It's coming. It'll be a day when you're so hurt that you cry yourself to sleep. So blinded by your lack that you can't see where your family's next meal is coming from. So angry that you're afraid you might loose your mind over a backstabbing. Yes, there are heartbreaks that leave you wondering if you can get out of bed. Physical ailments that make you question why you, why now and why God allowed it. These are the low times.

I've had my share of seasons when I felt like life kicked me when I was already down. That no matter how hard I tried to release the pain's discomforting grip of the day, I couldn't escape. The cascade of worry-filled thoughts, overflowing emotions or bad news was all encompassing.

One such moment was a summer I would never forget. My job had a major reduction in pay, but my bill collectors didn't really care. Neither did my appliances, apparently. The washer died and a month later the refrigerator decided to join his fellow appliance-man in the after life. But wait, there's more. Our car decided to blow a gasket, literally. It had the nerve to blow a head gasket while we were in no mans land on a family vacation. But this wasn't the first time this car abandoned its responsibility of being dependable. You see, three hundred and sixty five days prior to this breakdown the car was repaired for the same reason, but it decided to die one day after the warranty expired. Yes, we had savings, but nowhere near enough to save us. We found ourselves needing all our appliances repaired, a new car and an increase in overall income. This was a financial low time.

My wife and I didn't want to incur more debt. Lord knows we didn't need that nor could we afford it. I can't lie to you; the lack of money and how to get more of it became my focus. My problems consumed my mind. We were stuck and honestly I just wanted God to drop money from Heaven and get us out of this valley then life would be beautiful again. The sun would shine brighter and alas we would be happy. It seemed in that season it wasn't meant to be. I'm sure someone else was rejoicing over miracles on the other side of town, but this was our season for a low time for a life lesson.

The Furnace of Affliction

It's vital that you open your ears and shut your mouth in these moments of testing. You should open your ears because it may be a time of teaching, beyond the emotional storms of frustrations. Way deeper than the boundaries of discomfort may lay a blessing of promotion. Growth, in understanding wisdom from this experience and an increase in perspective, can be yours if you pause to listen to The Lord in the low times.

What seems to be a disaster for destructions sake may actually become the excavation site for the construction of YOU. I worked in construction for many years and as we would prepare to build a home on a new plot of land we'd begin with leveling the land. Digging up tree stumps, removing debris and digging into the soil to prepare it for the laying of a foundation. Without a firm foundation, the framing would eventually collapse. This process didn't look pretty, in fact it was messy and things were being moved all over the place. What was once an undisturbed, luscious green grass was now a muddy mess, but it was also a necessary and a strategic mess. It was part of a bigger plan for a stable home.

"But who will be able to stand up to that coming? Who can survive his appearance? He'll be like white-hot fire from the smelter's furnace. He'll be like the strongest lye soap at the laundry. He'll take his place as a refiner of silver, as a cleanser of dirty clothes. He'll scrub the Levite priests clean, refine them like gold and silver, until they're fit for GOD, fit to present offerings of righteousness. Then, and only then, will Judah and Jerusalem be fit and pleasing to GOD, as they used to be in the years long ago."

Malachi 3:2-4 MSG

The Prophet Malachi looks ahead to the coming of The Messiah. This book prepares the people for what's to come. He's still the same today as He was when this prophecy was fulfilled over 2000 years ago. What these verses give us are a snapshot of His nature and His methodology. For those He loves He purifies and refines.

Most of us aren't familiar with iron work. We haven't seen the smelters furnace blaze with the heat from intense fire. The fire gets turned up so intensely that the silver and gold undergoes a purifying process. The dross or impurities are separated from the precious metal.

Similarly, He takes the strongest lye soap to scrub clean His people. This reminds of my time as a construction worker. After a hard day's work our hands would be filthy. So dirty that regular hand soap would not clean the mess. We'd always keep Orange Soap around; this soap felt like rocks were embedded within the lather and our hands would definitely come out clean after the rocky discomfort.

Just as any litter found within the precious metal must go, sin within our hearts, pride or doubt has to go. We may not be aware of the hidden impurities of insecurity or core lies that need to be uprooted, but He sees it all and scrubs it off. He loves us enough to turn up life's heat to refine our hearts.

As Malachi prophesied to the people, we discovered that they pridefully justified themselves before God. Despite their many flaws and constant compromise, they defended their actions. The impurities within them had corrupted their worship and undoubtedly their ways of life as well. God in His mercy said Help was on the way. Unwilling to leave them in their sinful darkness, He would lead them to the light. Yet, He knew they would end up in rebellion because of the corruption of their hearts. To reach the heart, he'd turn up the heat and break out the soap.

King Solomon was one of the wisest men who ever lived. He also spoke about this technique of purifying the silver, *"Remove the impurities from silver, and the sterling will be ready for the silversmith." Proverbs 25:4 NLT* This is how God does it! Whether we like it or not and regardless if it feels good to us, I know it works for our good. We've got to learn from these life lessons so that we can graduate to the next level. Pure, shiny and squeaky clean.

This could indeed be that moment for you. It may not be beautiful but it is necessary for your growth. It's paramount for your progression to the next level of leading in life. As you walk with God He shapes you for the purpose in which He created you. Some situations are allowed to teach you now for the purpose of a greater later. So, you must put your ear to God's chest and inquire. What are You revealing about me? Lord, what are You teaching me about You through this? These are the questions we should ask or something similar to this line of thought. Often times we are so ready to get out of the low time, that we never grasp the purpose for which we came in. No more going around the same mountain!

Learn the lesson; pass the test now so you won't have to go through this class again.

Become a student of hearing, listening and learning. One way to do this is to journal your way through the low times. Every night ask yourself, "what happened to me today?" Write out about three sentences that get to the heart of incidents that stood out to you. Good or bad. Ask yourself, "How did this event affect my attitude about God, myself or other people?" Write out any negative impressions the injury had on your heart. Is there a lie that's being projected about God, yourself or others that need to be uprooted before going to sleep? Then write out the truth of God's word over your situation. A great resource that goes in depth with a thorough process for this is "Who switched off my brain", by Dr. Caroline Leaf.

Another key element of making it through while learning the lesson is to take one step at a time. My older brother had a stroke a few years back. It rocked our entire family to its core. For a moment we thought we'd lost him. One night he stopped breathing and lost consciousness after passing out. Miraculously he pulled through a really scary and life threatening low time. When he came to, his speech was impaired and the right side of his body was immobile. It was hard for me to even watch my brother in this position. I can only imagine what it was like for him to suffer through this trying time. Wanting to do simple things and unable to accomplish the task. He managed to gain some of his speech back within a couple of days. One of the things he said was a loud 'amen' at the end of one of the prayers we prayed with him as a family. Talk about faith in the face of adversity!

Another thing he said was, it was strange for him to be going through this paralysis because he would think to move his leg with his mind, but it wouldn't happen physically. Yet, he was determined to fight to regain his mobility.

When I was a kid I looked up to him for many reasons. One cool fact about him is that he was a boxer and wrestler growing up. He was great at fighting to say the least. As we sat in that hospital room I saw the fighter return to the ring. Fighting his way back from an ugly low time in his life. He had overcome so much in his life already. This was the next fight and I'm glad to say, he emerged as a champ. He regained his mobility, maybe not at the pace he wanted, but step-by-step he bounced back from the brink of death. One step at a time, he emerged to the point that his speech had returned and he was even able to drive again.

I don't know how hard life has hit you or what specific details surround your low time, but you can bounce back from a low blow at a low time. Just take it slow, one step at a time, listening and learning. Journaling your thoughts and ridding yourself of regrets and "why me's." Strengthening the champion within you with the truth of God's faithfulness. With everything that's within you, let there be a resounding amen!

Lesson Learned

Back to the low time during the summer when I faced the financial fire, I have learned that I'd been passive in planning for the worst. My wife and I had saved up to a certain point and then became complacent. We were financially comfortable while the cash was coming in. We saved up enough for a small shower but not enough for a major storm, let alone a hurricane. Since then we've raised the standard of saving. We've set financial goals and put plans in place to attain them. We have multiple streams of income because that's what we believe God has instructed us to do.

Now that we are out of the hurricane and have recovered all, we understand. We see differently and we've grown to a new level of financial discipline. It has impacted our family legacy. Our children have learned the truth about debt freedom and our church has as well. From experience we can tell others how to prepare for the low times by saving in the high times.

Now, what is God saying to you in this season? Journal it. Grow from it. If you have a mile to go to get to the end of this season, which direction should you take the next step in?

4. From Weeping To Refreshing

"We were promised sufferings. They were part of the program. We were even told, 'Blessed are they that mourn,' and I accept it. I've got nothing that I hadn't bargained for. Of course it is different when the thing happens to oneself, not to others, and in reality, not imagination."
C.S. Lewis, A Grief Observed

My wife and I had just moved to Texas from Indianapolis, Indiana with our two children. Brandon was three and Brianna was two at the time. We packed up our few possessions and moved to Fort Worth, Texas where I was hired to lead worship with a new church family. Honestly, Fort Worth wasn't my style, but we believed that's where God wanted us to be and so we looked forward to fresh start.

We welcomed this transition because Indianapolis was a rough experience to say the least. We only lived there for about a year, but it felt like the longest year of our lives. The list of spiritual, physical and financial attacks would be another book in itself. It felt like a Job season of affliction for us. When everything that could go wrong did go wrong.

During our time in Indiana, my wife went through a difficult season of sickness. The doctors couldn't figure out what was wrong with her or how to fix it. For several months this physical ailment persisted. The doctors couldn't identify the source of the problem or a solution, so we needed a miracle from God. We decided to trust God for healing. I believed that if He could heal Job, He could heal my wife. We stood in faith and just laid hands on her and declared the promises of God over her life. Through God's grace, she was healed after we fervently prayed and believed Him to do it. We experienced the power of faith and prayer first-hand. For us, there's no denying God's healing ability. Jesus healed the sick in the Bible days and He still does today.

Her sickness was just one of several problems we had. We had two cars break down and die within eight months; so, we were without a vehicle for a while. What looked like a promising opportunity for us in a new city, turned into a crushing blow in every way imaginable. When the cars went out, so did my job opportunities. There was little grace for an employee with unreliable transportation, so we became masters of the transit system. We would have to catch the bus throughout the city to get to work and everywhere else we needed to be.

One of the homes we lived in wasn't in the best neighborhoods to say the least. While I was working the nightshift at Fedex, my wife was at home with our children. Now, keep in mind this was before cell phone connectivity. If I wanted to call home to check in on her I would have to use the companies phone line. That particular night was terrifying for her. The tenants next door were engaged in a shooting and someone was actually shot. Sirens were blazing and cops were everywhere. I was powerless to do anything about it and she couldn't leave the house either. I arrived home after taking the bus, and being stressed out the entire time. Despite the fact that we were afraid, frustrated and worried, we praised God that our family was safe.

We fell on our knees and cried out to God for direction. We needed a breakthrough! First the sickness threatened my wife's life and now gunshots firing off in the room next door to my family. Is this what you wanted for us God? Why was this happening? It seemed like we couldn't catch a break… but then it got worse.

My wife's father Joseph who was battling colon cancer received the news that it was spreading throughout his body. He was given a few months to live at best. We had to move back to St. Louis so that we could spend quality time with him. We loved him, cared for him and prayed for a turnaround.

He was a great man. He walked with God in faith all the way through to his last breath. At that time we just didn't understand certain things. We had seen God do miracles for others and even for us when my wife was healed, but in his case, it seemed the prayers weren't reaching Heaven. It's as if God didn't get the memo. Surely, God could've healed him and raised him off his sick bed, but instead, Joseph went on to be with The Lord.

This moment in time was tough. In all honesty, this didn't even scratch the surface of all that we had gone through in this stretch of time while in Indianapolis, but lets fast forward a few months ahead to the move to Fort Worth. As you can imagine, we were ready for a change, yet another traumatic experience was on the horizon.

Give me that Good News!

After getting settled in Fort Worth, we found out Lanette was pregnant again. We were now expecting our third child. Despite the pressure that we were under with the transition to a new state, we welcomed the news. Raising children is a passion within our marriage's purpose so this news was good news.

A few months into the pregnancy we headed to the doctors office for an ultrasound. That's when we received even more good news. My wife was pregnant with twins! This, my friends was a shocker! Our families don't have many sets of twins running around on either side, so it would take us a moment to wrap our heads around the idea of having four children.

All kinds of thoughts began to race through our heads, like money. Instantly we knew a bigger budget was going to be a necessity along with putting a larger home on the list as well. Would they be two boys or girls, or could the twins be a boy and a girl? What should we name them? When will we break the news to the family? And all of a sudden, shock turned into rejoicing. There was so much excitement and anticipation over what was to come. Twins were coming! Or, so we thought. About six weeks into the pregnancy my wife knew that something was wrong after some spotting took place. We rushed to the nearest hospital and I'll never forget the moment after this ultrasound when we'd received the news that one of the twins died. She had a miscarriage.

We were both so heartbroken. More questions came. We were concerned about what happened to the other child in the womb? And was my wife's body in danger? We hadn't processed the loss of the baby, who we were so anxious to meet just moments ago. And just like that, they stabilized my wife and we were leaving the hospital. In shock over the disappointing news, we were upset and hurt, yet again.

We didn't say much about it to one another. In fact, it wasn't until a good friend of ours, Louis, who was giving us a ride home, began to speak about it. He shared words of encouragement and words to us about grief. My wife and I sat there in his suburban listening to him, gazing out of the window as we began to weep. Tears flowed as we processed our pain and began to mourn the loss of our unborn child.

Maybe you're in a time of mourning. Do you weep for the loss of a loved one? Is your heart weighted down with the heaviness of grief? We all have moments of mourning, but they should be just that, moments. Grieving the loss of a loved one, wealth or health temporarily is human. To accept it as a lifestyle however, is tragic. Depression, hopelessness and fear will become the norm in the life of a believer stuck in the rut of grief. I feel your pain and we pray for your mourning to be turned to gladness.

How to Overcome a Season of Grief

The prophet Isaiah gave us a powerful word of encouragement. He expounded on Jesus, The Anointed One, who came to set the captives free. Christ came to heal the broken hearted and restore vision to those who've lost their sight. Our hope for healing is found in Jesus alone. He wills to repair our broken hearts from the greatest hurt and tragic disasters. Things will get better! You will recover and your life will go on.

"To console those who mourn in Zion,
To give them beauty for ashes, The oil of joy for mourning,
The garment of praise for the spirit of heaviness;
That they may be called trees of righteousness,
The planting of the Lord, that He may be glorified." Isaiah 61:3 (NKJV)

This verse gives voice to the truth that mourning **can** end and joy can begin. We don't have to remain in the shadows of grief. God wants to comfort His people during and after tragic moments of our lives that leave us in the ashes of ruin. In those moments where we don't understand why He allowed the unthinkable. Yet, He promises to be with us and strengthen us from within to withstand the grief.

Jesus understands our pain. He walked in this world as a man just like us. He felt sorrows and was acquainted with grief, so Jesus can relate. As we face traumatic experiences we can transparently pray through the pain. We can lift up the ashes from the ruins of our reality and God himself will exchange the ashes for beauty.

Some people say, time heals all wounds, but that's not true. Time in fact may fortify the sickness that's festering with an open wound. Jesus is the healer of the broken hearted. You see, ashes in the bible days represented mourning. Zion represented God's chosen people, the Jews. At the time of this prophetic passage, the Jewish people had suffered so much grief and persecution. This has remained throughout human history. From slavery in Egypt to the Holocaust, they know what mourning is. This prophetic word proclaimed that Messiah's anointing was so great that it could exchange that level of horrific grief for beauty. He will place the oil of gladness of the heads of those whose minds are troubled by the terror of loss. The days of mourning will end. A new day of restoration is available to us if we are willing to receive it.

The promise in verse three lets us know there will be a transformation. A garment of praise will replace the spirit of heaviness. This praise garment was a festive ceremonial garment. It would be exchanged for the sackcloth and ashes over the years of mourning. This is a metaphor for a spiritual reality. There will be such a spiritual transformation within your heart that your language changes. Your mind is renewed and your outlook on life becomes one of praise instead of depression.

How does this take place?

When life hits you in the gut with a sucker punch, it hurts! Believers aren't impervious to feeling. Denying the reality of what we experience emotionally, mentally or physically only lengthens the effects of the blow. Faith doesn't negate feeling and its ok to acknowledge it.

If you're feeling sad, own that. Are thoughts of depression dominating your mind? Have doubts about God's love for you surfaced due to your suffering? Do you feel alone as you're walking through a life crisis? Then admit what you're feeling. After all, you can't heal a wound by saying its not there.

"My people are broken--shattered! --and they put on Band-Aids, Saying, 'It's not so bad. You'll be just fine.
'But things are not 'just fine'![1]"
Jeremiah 6:13-14 (The Message)

One of the biggest mistakes in the process of healing is denying the need for restoration. You may need to make the investment to see a professional counselor in the aftermath of a disaster. Don't try to suppress your brokenness. Internally, as Jeremiah put it, you're shattered! Why slap a band-aid on top of a gunshot wound to the soul? Come on my friend, how bad is it?

That divorce may have caused more hurt than you're letting on. You may need heart surgery because of it. Again, don't put a band-aid on it. The miscarriages may have altered your perspective on yourself, your spouse or of God... Get help! Professional counseling doesn't mean that you're defective. It means you're wise enough to know the power of community. There's strength in talking it out with someone who can see within.

In times of depression, confusion or sadness we tend to want to be alone, and that may be okay for a brief moment, but isolation leaves you susceptible to a perpetuation of negative thoughts and unhealthy emotions. We as human beings need people. We need to release our grief and we also need others to encourage us.

The Valley of Weeping

"What joy for those whose strength comes from the Lord, who have set their minds on a pilgrimage to Jerusalem. When they walk through the Valley of Weeping, it will become a place of refreshing springs. The autumn rains will clothe it with blessings. They will continue to grow stronger, and each of them will appear before God in Jerusalem."
Psalm 84:5–7 (NLT)

Within *Psalm 84:5-7* we find keys to turning the valley of weeping into refreshing springs. Our sorrows will convert to joy as with *Isaiah 61:3*. There's a divine empowerment that comes from the Lord, but this divine healing flows to those who have made up in their minds to journey to Jerusalem.

When this passage was written, people went on annual pilgrimages to Jerusalem to worship. It was a journey to "appear before God." As their minds focused on getting closer to God they grew stronger in joy. This is a beautiful picture of what happens when we determine within ourselves to pursue God despite the problems. Getting closer to the Lord through our valleys of weeping leads to supernatural strength. Could it be that suffering could work to bring us closer to God?

Have you noticed that during funerals we become temporarily awakened to the fragility of life? Our thoughts process spiritual realities of life eternal on a heightened level. We are open to trust God beyond the realm of the senses. Faith, hope and the comforting words of God are our recourse. After all, the matters of life after death are beyond our control. In these moments, we must trust that our loved ones lives are in His hands; this is how we seek solace in The Savior. Somehow our sadness turns into laughter as we remember the sweet memories of our loved ones. Hugs and words of encouragement fill the reception halls and as family laugh and fellowship at the repast, we witness weeping turn into refreshing right before our eyes.

This passage becomes even more powerful as we dig deeper into the meaning of Jerusalem. Jerusalem translates as the City of Peace. It's considered to be God's Holy city. One day the Messiah will rule on the earth from that very place. Jesus' name is the Prince of Peace. Maybe that's why there's so much turmoil surrounding that city. There's been unceasing warfare over that territory for thousands of years. The city of peace has seen its share of chaos. Even so, it has withstood the attacks against it.

We must pursue the city of peace. In other words, don't give up on your peace of mind in the world of turmoil. Get to God when the world tries to get to you. Peace will stand amongst the ever-increasing attacks against it. And as you pursue peace in God, your joy will increase and your strength will be restored. The valley of weeping and the tears you've shed along the way will become as a refreshing spring. You will be clothed with blessings in exchange for a season that seemed cursed.

Even Jesus faced evil while He was in this world. The ugliness of sin and the falling away of the world was laid on Him and He completely ingested it within Himself. The Prince of Peace prevailed against our greatest pains. Christ can create comfort within our calamity. Peace within our greatest storms. Giving us courage to face our fears. You will prevail as you pursue the presence of God.

Clothed in Blessing

Isaiah 61 proclaimed the Good News that Messiah would turn times of mourning into times of praise. The Psalmist told us that the valley of weeping would turn into times of refreshing. Jesus himself had something to say about mourning as well. As He's giving the famous beatitudes, He gives us a promise that we can hold on to.

"God blesses those who mourn, for they will be comforted."
Matthew 5:4 (NLT)

The word Makarios is the Greek translation of blessed or happy. When Jesus says, "God bless," it can be translated as God gives empowerment for happiness to those who are mourning. He will empower all who come to Him for comfort with a garment of praise in the valley of weeping. He will exchange our sadness for comfort. Supernaturally He can console us through it all. This is our promise. If you're in a valley of weeping, get a grip on this promise from Jesus. Build your hope on the Word of God.

I encourage you to turn towards Heaven and cast your cares on Him for He cares for you. Don't carry what you should've cast into His care. The disappointment, the unanswered questions and all the pain must be given to God. In exchange, He will grant you peace. You will be blessed. Somehow, divine satisfaction will be greater than the grief.

Jesus said that He would give us peace that cannot be taken away. As The Prince of Peace, He rules over an endless supply of shalom. This harmony can replace discord and wholeness will fill the fragmented. He came for this purpose! He will do His part, but you and I, by faith must do our part. We must come to Him in our moments of mourning.

"Don't worry about anything; instead, pray about everything. Tell God what you need, and thank him for all he has done. 7 Then you will experience God's peace, which exceeds anything we can understand. His peace will guard your hearts and minds as you live in Christ Jesus."
Philippians 4:6–7 (NLT)

The Apostle Paul gives us inspired instructions for acquiring this blessed peace. Stop worrying about what you can't control. Don't stress over what you can- not change. In place of worry, insert prayer. For everything that is on your heart, tell God what you need. I once heard a great preacher, Bishop John Wade say, take your hands off of it and put your knees on it.

His divine grace then enables you to praise through the pain. In fact, praise Him in everything. You may not want to praise God for everything that happen because something's aren't praise worthy, but your God is. Having an attitude of gratitude changes your altitude. Instead of focusing on all that's gone wrong, praise Him for all that is right. Sometimes we have nothing to be grateful for because we have no one to be grateful to.

In turning to God, you'll discover that you have reasons to praise Him. Though my wife and I went through heartbreaking loss and setbacks, we made it. Her father lived a great life. We thanked God for that. He was ready to be with the Father and we will see Him again. We thanked God for that.

We still had a beautiful and vibrant baby girl. Despite being born prematurely and the miscarriage of the other baby, she made it. We praise God for her. We also rejoice because life begins at conception. For our unborn child, we look forward to the day that we will see you in heaven. We thank God for an amazing family reunion in glory.

When our prayers and praise outweigh our pain, then we experience God's peace. That's His promise! Our hearts and minds are the seat of our emotions, passions and desires. When our hearts are sick due to hopes and dreams deferred, the peace of God will stand guard to calm the storms of disappointment. The peace of God bypasses our understanding of how it happens and makes joy override our sadness.

We don't have to know how God does it, but we have to trust that He does. He will wipe every tear from our eyes. One day there will be no more suffering and no need for mourning. Death, sin and sickness will be done away with in the life to come. Until that day, while we live in this world, there will be suffering. And though there's suffering, there's also a Savior. He's here to help us when our hearts hurt in the valley of weeping.

5. Satisfaction in The Savior

"God is most glorified in us when we are most satisfied in Him" ~ John Piper

I can remember on that blessed day called Thanksgiving, eating until the point when I couldn't eat any longer. I had eaten of the goodness of the chef and the provision of my parents until I had more than enough. Full, completely satisfied and content. There's a contentment that David expresses in Psalm 23 that we must receive as well. Listen to this promise from God himself to His children:

"...be satisfied with what you have. For God has said, 'I will never fail you. I will never abandon you.' So we can say with

confidence, 'The Lord is my helper, so I will have no fear. What can mere people do to me?'" Hebrews 13:5–6 (NLT)

Is your hunger for God greater than your quest for an answer from God? Is your need of Him greater than your wants from Him? I've lost sight of seeking God throughout the difficult moments of my life. I used prayer as a tool to get things from God, instead of having genuine conversations with God to receive Him. I pursued blessings from my Heavenly Father, but wasn't maintaining a true relationship with Him. Don't get me wrong, there are times when we should request what we need in prayer to our Father, but there should be meaningful conversations outside of wants and requests. Can you imagine having a relationship with a child who only comes to you when they want things from you? You see, a good parent loves to give to their children, so there's a joy when they trust you to meet their needs. Still, a parent longs to have an intimate relationship with their child. God welcomes our request and prayers but He also offers us access to Himself, and that is the greatest blessing of all.

Remember this, we become what we behold the most. God offers us the satisfaction of beholding His presence because we have a covenant relationship. He offers us the ability to absorb our identity from Him. There's a satisfaction that is in The Savior alone. A fulfillment that can't be ascertained in the finitude of this world. Finality means there's an expiration date. There's a loaf of bread purchased that only stays fresh for so long. It's only of use to you for a moment; it provides temporary sustenance. It's like a good Thanksgiving meal; it satisfies you, but the next day you'll need leftovers. You crave more because as soon as it's out of your system and you continue to eat it for a few days...it gets boring and eventually spoils.

Sadly, this is what people's relationship with God looks like. Sunday we eat the feast. We eat a huge chunk of Jesus and try to live off of that experience for the rest of the week. No wonder people fall for the temptations of this world, they are in great need of their daily bread! You see, we need to return to Him each day. You need Him like the air you breathe. You realize that without His presence, you can't make it! So, are you truly satisfied with Jesus? Or, do you believe you need a certain possession to be happy? To be satisfied in your life right now, 'what's the dollar amount?' Don't fall for it! Only Jesus can satisfy the hunger of life because only He is life itself:

"Jesus replied, I am the bread of life. Whoever comes to me will never be hungry again. Whoever believes in me will never be thirsty."
John 6:35 (NLT)

He's calling for us to feast on Him. How in the world do we do that? Well, a clue is within the verse above. Believing in Jesus to be your Savior is the key. Another way to say that would be to declare today that Jesus is your salvation. He's your escape from judgment and condemnation. Jesus is your ticket to freedom over bondage. Jesus is your protection in the flames. Jesus is your resurrection from the grave.

In Hebrews 13:5 the word for 'satisfied' in the Greek is arkeo (ἀρκεο). It means, "to be possessed of unfailing strength, to suffice, to be enough." Let's bring that to an applicable level. When we are Jesus dependent we posses unfailing strength. We have all sufficiency. We have enough within us to overcome difficulty in life.

Rely on The Holy Spirit within you no matter what obstacles surround you. Whenever you face these hurdles outside of you, be sure to remember who you need inside of you. The flesh leans to finite resources. We tend to trust in material things in times of trouble, but there's greater power in the person of Jesus than we can imagine. If we reach to Him by faith, He will prove Himself to be more than enough to pick us up and carry us through.

> *"...Be satisfied with what you have. For God has said, "I will never fail you. I will never abandon you." 6 So we can say with confidence, "The Lord is my helper, so I will have no fear. What can mere people do to me?"*
> *Hebrews 13:5–6 (NLT)*

If you are under attack and feel fear, acknowledge it. Denying fear doesn't help you to overcome it. We all will be tempted with fear. Now, it's one thing to be tempted to fear, it's another thing to succumb to the temptation. So, how do we overcome fear and anxiety? This verse reveals a clue that can assist us in overcoming the spirit of fear. He has said to you personally this day, "I will never fail you. I will never abandon you."

What that means in the Greek language is actually stronger than our English translation of the text. It's more like God's personal guarantee that's been hand delivered to us. The word "leave" in this passage is more than Him walking away from your side. The word leave is *aniemi*: to send back, to loosen, to let sink. In other words, God is saying, "I won't allow you to sink!" Hear God's voice today, "I will not allow you to be released from my care and provision."

The word, forsake, is a combination of words in the Greek (eg-kata-leipo). Eg means "in", Kata meaning defeat, or helplessness and leipo meaning "to leave". The idea is that God doesn't leave you helpless in your hardship. He doesn't bail when the ship is about to sink! He's a true friend that sticks closer than a brother. He is a real Dad who'll always be around in your life. He's the kind of Father that you can build your hopes on and He won't "reject you!"

Have you faced rejection from the people you've called on in times of trouble? If you have, then you know it hurts deeply. Some of you have been violated by people who were close to you. That violation may have been physical or even sexual abuse. In other situations, family neglected you. And possibly, in your time of need, friends ignored you. Well, your Heavenly Father will never reject you. "I won't abandon you or desert you", He promised. He will not, ever, ever leave you helpless. Now, I know that is not grammatically correct, but that is how it reads in the Greek. The promise carries the idea of a "triple promise" from God! It's like God saying, "I won't, I won't ever, I will never abandon you in your moment of helplessness and difficult circumstances." He will come to your rescue.

This is why we shouldn't be afraid. The Good Shepherd who provides restoration for our souls is with us. Yahweh is here to be our provision. That's better than the money you think you need. Greater than the friends or family you wish you had. He can heal you where you've been hurt and restore to you what's been lost.

You may have a person who's persecuting you because of your faith on campus. Or, a coworker is plotting against you on your job. Listen, don't be afraid of what man can do to you when you know what God has done for you. Don't be afraid of someone spreading rumors about you. Why pay attention to their words when you have a relationship with The Word! Why worry about the threats of man when you can rejoice in the promises of God. You see, this is what it means to be satisfied with Jesus. You don't need the applause of man when God approves you. Faith says that no matter what people or possessions come or go, I have all that I need. There's a spiritual blessing that satisfies my soul and it's someone greater than gold, God Himself.

Now some may say that they don't get why that's enough. I'll put it like this...if a billionaire was on his deathbed in a hospital room, do you think his Bentley matters then? He can't take the money or possessions with him. Especially if he has no one to give it to after he's gone. If he's on that bed alone with no one to comfort him, no one to look forward to seeing again in the next life, then that's a pretty lonely existence. It's not good for mankind to live alone. We weren't designed to live that way. We aren't designed to live life apart from our source of life more than anything.

C.S. Lewis said: *"If we find ourselves with a desire that nothing in this world can satisfy, the most probable explanation is that we were made for another world."*

Please understand that I'm not against prosperity in this world. There's nothing wrong with prospering in this life. Search the scriptures and you'll discover that God constantly prospered His people. However, God's people would turn material possessions into idols. To show the futility of worshiping material things, God turned them over to the idols that they worshipped. They'd discover that without God's provision, left to themselves and false gods, they were helpless.

What I'm saying is, we can't allow wealth to become what we worship. We shouldn't rise and fall as our possessions or people increase or decrease. There's nothing wrong with having possessions, but something's wrong when our focus or our faith is in anything but The King.

If this has happened then we must repent. To repent is to get a new way of thinking. What's that new way of thinking? It says, I'm satisfied with Jesus. What does this kind of faith look like? Let's take a look at the words of The Apostle Paul:

"How I praise the Lord that you are concerned about me again. I know you have always been concerned for me, but you didn't have the chance to help me. Not that I was ever in need, for I have learned how to be content with whatever I have. I know how to live on almost nothing or with everything. I have learned the secret of living in every situation, whether it is with a full stomach or empty, with plenty or little. For I can do everything through Christ, who gives me strength."
Philippians 4:10–13 (NLT)

When Paul was preaching the gospel the local church wanted to support him monetarily, but they couldn't in this instance for whatever reason. Paul said in essence, "You know my physical needs". That's why they wanted to give to him but something prevented them from being able to meet his need. Yet, Paul didn't react out of bitterness nor did he panic under pressure. Instead he tells us that he wasn't ever in need. Now, you and I both know that every human being needs resources. The message here is, that on Paul's journey of preaching God's message, he was never alone. Meaning, if one channel of blessing closed in the natural, doesn't mean every channel is closed. It doesn't mean heaven has lost its only option. God was with him. Now check out what Paul "learned." He learned contentment...satisfaction with Jesus. No matter what he physically possessed he was confident that what he had need of, God was always supplying.

He gives further clarity in verse 12, *"I know how to live on almost nothing or with everything."* The secret to living no matter what comes or goes is living your life through the provision of Christ. Jesus' grace is more than theological rhetoric. His grace is attainable and transformative. Grace is God's divine ability to endure whatever hits you in life. It's God's personal power that strengthens you.

This power is available to you right now. How's that possible you ask? Well, He promised to never leave you. Take Him to the place of your lack. Tell Him, come and see where my problem lay. Watch the grace of God give life in your times of lack and even in your times of plenty.

6. Security Under Siege

"Limits, like fear, is often an illusion."
- Michael Jordan

Our source of security, provision and victory is the Trinity; God our Father, Jesus our Savior, and The Holy Spirit dwelling within us. One God, manifest in three ways. This oneness of The Trinity is a mystery within God's majesty. In Genesis, the Book of Beginnings, we sit at the throne of God and watch His power at work during creation. We see the Trinity in unity and yet we are aware of His diversity.

"In the beginning God created the heavens and the earth. The earth was formless and empty, and darkness covered the

deep waters. And the Spirit of God was hovering over the surface of the waters. Then God said, "Let there be light," and there was light."
Genesis 1:1–3 (NLT)

There are several nuggets that'll strengthen our faith in this passage. One thought comes to mind; you and I would do well to keep God at the beginning. Keep God as the focus of your worship, your reason for being or at the beginning of your decision-making. Another thought is, keep God at the start. At the start of your next counseling session let God take the lead. While planning your finances, put God first. If you're making any sort of life plans, may God's input be at the beginning. How can you go wrong in life when you acknowledge God at the start of all your ways?

We see the Trinity at work from the beginning. God creates, the Spirit moves and The Word is spoken. God the Father is like a composer who creates in harmony with His counsel. He creates through His Word. The question isn't which word, but Who is the word. Check out these verses of Truth:

"In the beginning the Word already existed. The Word was with God, and the Word was God. He existed in the beginning with God. God created everything through him, and nothing was created except through him. The Word gave life to everything that was created and his life brought light to everyone."
John 1:1–4 (NLT)

Note: the Word **was** God and yet was **with** God and note: the Word **gave** life to everything that was created. Jesus is the Word! Jesus is active in giving life to all creation. Jesus is in harmony with God the Father. The good news is that Jesus continues to give life to everyone who's willing to receive Him.

"Humans can reproduce only human life, but the Holy Spirit gives birth to spiritual life. So don't be surprised when I say, 'You must be born again.' The wind blows wherever it wants. Just as you can hear the wind but can't tell where it comes

from or where it is going, so you can't explain how people are born of the Spirit." John 3:6–8 (NLT)

The Holy Spirit was moving upon the face of the waters. We don't have enough space in this book to cover the amazing person of the Holy Spirit, but He's God on earth residing within us. He empowers us with godly character and spiritual fruit. He transforms us into the image of Jesus Christ. He is as essential to the human body as water is to the material world. Interestingly enough, the Holy Spirit is metaphorically referenced to as The River of Living water.

"On the last day, the climax of the festival, Jesus stood and shouted to the crowds, 'Anyone who is thirsty may come to me! Anyone who believes in me may come and drink! For the Scriptures declare, 'Rivers of living water will flow from his heart.'"
John 7:37–39 (NLT)

When He said *"living water,"* He was speaking of the Spirit, who would be given to everyone believing in

Him. However, the Spirit had not been given yet, because Jesus had not entered into His glory.

As Jesus is teaching we come to a point of awe and wonder and at the same time yet mind stretching frustration. For He's one with The Father and yet speaks also of being sent from the Father to do His will.

"While Jesus was teaching in the Temple, he called out, "Yes, you know me, and you know where I come from. But I'm not here on my own. The One who sent me is true, and you don't know him. But I know him because I come from him, and he sent me to you."
John 7:28–29 (NLT)

This looks like the pattern established in the beginning. God the Father sends the Word and The Spirit works where and when the Word was manifest. The Fathers intent is to create the material world from the spiritual reality. The spiritual reality was first and then the natural world came into existence. The unity of the Trinity at work on His God given intent leads us to the creation of all the material world. From His mystery we behold His majesty. From His majesty we behold the power of unity!

Perfect Security Under Siege.

Jesus knew who He was while He was in this world. He knew His roots, which led to Him understanding His rights. People in His own household rejected and mocked Him. People from the religious community wanted Him dead. He was despised and rejected by the very people he'd come to save. Still no matter how mankind attacked Him in this life, Jesus stayed rooted in the truth.

He walked in a reality that the men around Him couldn't see. When they looked at Him from a physical standpoint they saw a carpenters son from a small town, but when people saw the miracles that came from Him and the truths He revealed, they realized He was from out of this world. Jesus had perfect security when His life was under siege.

When we are enamored with tribulations and frustrations in life, we tend to loose focus. Often times we panic under pressure. Sometimes, we may find it difficult to persevere through the pain. Jesus managed to overcome and emerge triumphant in the face of tragedy. Let's observe The Word at work. Take a look at how He spoke to an angry mob of doubting Pharisees who wanted to kill Him.

"My sheep hear My voice, and I know them, and they follow Me. And I give them eternal life, and they shall never perish; neither shall anyone snatch them out of My hand. My Father, who has given them to Me, is greater than all; and no one is able to snatch them out of My Father's hand. I and My Father are one."

John 10:27–30 (NKJV)

"I and my Father are one!" Jesus owns the sheep and gives them life. He protects them from danger. It's the Father who gives the sheep to Him. He then brags of His Father, *"He's greater than all."* Jesus was in the world during this time in human form. People were threatening to kill him. I'd say that's a pretty difficult moment. I'd call

that a valley of the shadow of death. How did He keep His composure?

He knew His connection to the source of life through the unity of Trinity. He declared The Father was and is, greater than them all. I want to encourage you today, know that life is greater than death. You are in the hands of life Himself! Nothing can pluck you from God's hands, no matter how bad things appear in the physical realm, God is still in control.

Don't be distracted by the tactics of your adversary. Satan's goal is to get us to "feel" and "think" that we are alone in this world. It's not true. We are in the hands of Jesus Himself. Remember this as well; wherever you see the Word at work, the Spirit is moving. God has sent the Holy Spirit to live in us to confirm this truth. We are not alone! We are members of the family of God and that comes with benefits, but I'm getting ahead of myself. I'd like to dive deeper into the unity of the Trinity for a moment.

Jesus is the expression or unveiling of God Himself. Jesus is the exact personification of God the Father. When Jesus spoke of oneness with the Father, we are talking inseparable. The very Glory of God is Jesus Christ as stated in Hebrews 1:1-8.

God speaks to us through His Son and His Son speaks to us through His Spirit living within us. Jesus shares the throne of the Father in Heaven according to scripture. God saved the world through Christ Jesus.

Angels are stunning creatures. God made them to be celestial beings. They're made of a heavenly substance. Throughout scriptures angels would appear to men and their hearts would faint upon looking at an angel face to face. Yet, this passage declared the angels worship Jesus, the name that is greater than theirs. The angels are Jesus' ministering servants, who carry out His commands. Jesus is ruler and yet the Son of God.

Why is this important? You and I were created in the image of God Himself. God is majestic and so are we. When that life was snatched away at the fall of mankind, (See Gen. 3) God the Father gave us salvation through His Son. Not for the purpose of us becoming a religious moralist. He came to give us a new life, a life that's in harmony with a new spiritual reality. The reality that we are God's children and nothing can separate us from His life.

At creation, we see life being given to all created things. Yet, it's only human beings that receive the privilege of mirroring His image and likeness. As we've read these few passages of scripture we've observed that God is the source of life. The Son and Spirit give life. We are made in the image of life.

"Then God said, "Let Us make man in Our image, according to Our likeness; let them have dominion over the fish of the sea, over the birds of the air, and over the cattle, over all the earth and over every creeping thing that creeps on the

earth." So God created man in His own image; in the image of God He created him; male and female He created them. Then God blessed them, and God said to them, "Be fruitful and multiply; fill the earth and subdue it; have dominion over the fish of the sea, over the birds of the air, and over every living thing that moves on the earth."

Genesis 1:26–28 (NKJV)

God said, *"Let Us..."* The "Us" here is the Trinity. Some people have suggested the angels, but the angels aren't made in the image of God. They were created by God and for Him. Angels, simply put, aren't in the Holy counsel of the Trinity. He's referring to Himself: God The Father, God The Son and God The Holy Spirit. God manifested in three persons. Part of the mystery of His majesty is unity in diversity. Having the same mind at the same time.

Seeing Your Circumstance Through God's Eyes

Ok Sean, what does this have to do with getting through my valley? Well, what if you could have the mind of God? What if we could think the thoughts of God? What would those thoughts sound like? What could those thoughts do within us? Let's take a look at *1Cor 2:6-16*

What this scripture shows us is a mind-blowing benefit of receiving The Holy Spirit upon salvation. Every believer has access to the thoughts of God Himself. We can evaluate the realities of this world from the perspective of the One who created it. God, who was at the beginning of all we know in this material world, will download His eternal wisdom into your mind. Just as Christ was rooted in the reality of who He was and where He was from, we can become rooted in Christ. Jesus wasn't shaken in the natural because He rested in the spiritual truth. The perspective of God is the truth.

This wisdom from the mind of God is from His Spirit, to spiritual people. God even teaches us in complex mysteries. You can be more than a helpless human being under attack in this world. You can be more than a person going through tribulation after tribulation. You can be more than a helpless victim under attack by the kingdom of darkness. How can you become more than a victim?

By receiving the life that comes from God's Spirit. Check it again. Verse 10 said that The Spirit searches the depths of God. You have received His Spirit and He teaches you. You can understand the reality of who you are, right where you are. You can know within that God loves you no matter what you face. You can receive within you that nothing can pluck you from His hands. You can receive the reality within that God works all things together for good. Not just from reading those verses of text, but through encounters with The Holy Spirit, where He illuminates the truth within you. These become more than biblical text to memorize, but realities to live by.

They transform you. They root you in the reality of the super and it trumps the conditions of your natural.

As with Jesus, you can stand in the face of death itself and know to whom you belong! You can know fear when you see it and live without it. No fear here, because within us dwells the revelation of God's truth.

This is oneness with God; a unity with the Trinity, but not from a divine perspective. I'm not saying you are God with the Trinity, but you have been invited to be of the same family through grace. Access to an intimacy, relationally. You can live in harmony with the Trinity.

"Let us make mankind in our image," is the statement of the Trinity. We can resemble God or reflect God's glory. We aren't God and can't take His throne, but we can indeed mirror the image of God. Yes, we can reflect His character. As The Holy Spirit manifests the Son, the Son manifests the Father. You and I can manifest to the world the mind of God. You can be restored to the image or mirror of God.

Is God afraid? Is God defeated? Is God unholy? Of course not. The point is you and I can be in our current situations as a reflection of God. We can react through the Spirit's insight and power in the same manner God Himself would without fear, defeat or unrighteousness.

When I say that you aren't alone, I'm not merely suggesting you are by yourself. I'm speaking of real potency over your problems. You aren't impotent when you're empowered by the Omnipotent God.

In Genesis we watch the universe come to be as the thoughts of God are shared and carried out through His Word and Spirit. When God released His Word, His light dispelled the darkness. Everything in creation became good in God's eyes. What if your world was all-good in God's eyes? Maybe it is! Could it be that what we see with our natural eyes isn't all there is? What is to come is greater than what's been. This moment will become a building block in your character. Your trials are drawing you closer to the Father. Who knows? The Spirit does! And He can guide you in the Truth. If you desire security when your life is under siege, you'll need a reality of Heaven that supersedes what you experience on earth.

The enemy is projecting lies about you and about God, but if you're willing to keep your eyes on the Lord, you can move by faith instead of the fake. The truth is the reality of what's happening right now in your life. When the troubles of life hit us, we typically focus on the point of frustration or injury. We tend to focus on the problem, but I submit to you that the problem will pass. The key to making it through is remembering who's you are and who you are.

I know we've reviewed lots of scripture, and in all honesty, with each passage you can further the study on your own. If you do you'll discover nuggets that'll strengthen your faith. I'd like to add more truth from the text. John 17 to be exact. Jesus prays a prayer to The Father before His crucifixion. This is actually *"The Lord's Prayer."* When you have time, I encourage you to read this entire prayer. This is only a part of His words.

"I am praying not only for these disciples but also for all who will ever believe in me through their message. I pray that they will all be one, just as you and I are one--as you are in me, Father, and I am in you. And may they be in us so that the world will believe you sent me. I have given them the glory you gave me, so they may be one as we are one. I am in them and you are in me. May they experience such perfect unity that the world will know that you sent me and you love them as much as you love me.
John 17:20–23 (NLT)

Out of all the things Jesus could've prayed for, He requested to be one with the Father. He even prays that we experience the same type of unity that's found within the Trinity. He doesn't pray that we are removed from this world, but while we are here we'd know this oneness. The world would learn of Him through what we go through and how we go through it. The world, who doesn't know this God of love, will see a perfect unity on display between mankind and The Savior.

We can experience God's unconditional love in every condition of this life. What state is your heart in? What condition is your family in? What condition is this world in? We may not have a favorable answer to these questions, but if I may suggest for a moment, take your eyes off of the tragedy and depravity of this world and place your eyes on the beauty of Heaven within you. Focus less on the problems and hone in on the true solution. Whatever you focus your attention on dominates your perspective. Focus more on the mind of God within you and allow victory within to dominate the circumstances around you.

7. The Valley of Beracah

"We would worry less if we praised more. Thanksgiving is the enemy of discontent and dissatisfaction." - Harry Ironside

One day our church was redesigning the worship auditorium. Our team was installing lights, sound equipment and a projector screen. It was an "all hands on deck" type of moment. The projector screen came inside of a plastic case, but it was about fourteen feet wide and ten feet high. The parts for the legs and frame of the screen were metal. It was about one hundred pounds to lift. Nothing too heavy for me, right?

I reached down to move the case a few feet over. Again, nothing too heavy for me, but as I lifted the case and rotated my torso, I heard something pop. My back instantly got tight but I continued to work because it didn't seem like a big deal. Not too long after this incident, chronic back pain became a familiar experience. For a few months I lived with sharp and numb pains shooting through my back.

This continued until one day I woke up and got out of bed. Before I could take the first step, a pain so strong shot through my legs to my back. I fell to the floor and shouted in pain. My wife was there and ran over to assist me. You all must understand, I'm Mr. Tough Guy! I can take pain but that day I was as flimsy as a rag doll. It was excruciating and I had expressed it in every way imaginable. I had to explain to my wife what happened and how bad it felt. Grabbing the areas that hurt while grunting and making faces of frustration, I crawled my way onto the couch and used my wife as a crutch to get into the car and drove to the ER as fast as we could. My pain became the center of attention.

Can you relate to this? Experiencing intense pain beyond what I've described. Cancer creates unimaginable pain. The treatments for cancer are an entirely different battle. And the loss of a loved one is an emotional world of hurt as well. The betrayal of a friend or a spouse will leave a heart shattered in disbelief. Failing to reach your goals are another kind of pain. Financial ruin produces stress and money fights can leave families in disarray.

Our reactions are ways of releasing. Our responses communicate to God, others or ourselves the level of hurt we're facing. It speaks to the amount of help we need and in our retort to a threat on our wellbeing we react. Sometimes that reaction is a panic under pressure. It's a natural inclination to release in response to pain.

But what is the appropriate reaction in the face of adversity? After we've had our moment of humanness, what's our supernatural responsibility? I'd like to share with you the best way to get through a threat against you. When you're going through a valley that's attempting to take you out, or when the enemy of your soul seems to have the upper hand. In the moment that life hurts you the worst, here's what you should do the most. We must learn to let praise lead the way through pain.

We're going to dive into a powerful story of King Jehoshaphat. He was the leader of God's people at a time when armies had formed themselves against them. Now, these enemies meant business. They've come to take them out. The Moabites, Ammonites and the Meunites, came to fight against Judah. Jehoshaphat was wise enough to pray to God for direction. God gave him a word through a prophet that Judah would prevail. Let's see the Kings response in the time of war.

2 Chronicles 20:20–26 (HCSB)

20 In the morning they got up early and went out to the wilderness of Tekoa. As they were about to go out, Jehoshaphat stood and said, "Hear me, Judah and you inhabitants of Jerusalem. Believe in Yahweh your God, and you will be established; believe in His prophets, and you will succeed." 21 Then he consulted with the people and appointed some to sing for the Lord and some to praise the splendor of His holiness. When they went out in front of the armed forces, they kept singing: Give thanks to the Lord, for His faithful love endures forever.

22 The moment they began their shouts and praises, the Lord set an ambush against the Ammonites, Moabites, and the inhabitants of Mount Seir who came to fight against Judah, and they were defeated. 23 The Ammonites and Moabites turned against the inhabitants of Mount Seir and completely annihilated them. When they had finished with the inhabitants of Seir, they helped destroy each other.

24 When Judah came to a place overlooking the wilderness, they looked for the large army, but there were only corpses lying on the ground; nobody had escaped. 25 Then Jehoshaphat and his people went to gather the plunder. They found among them an abundance of goods on the bodies and valuable items. So they stripped them until nobody could carry any more. They were gathering the plunder for three days because there was so much. 26 They assembled in the Valley of Beracah on the fourth day, for there they praised the Lord. Therefore, that place is still called the Valley of Beracah today."

This is fascinating. Here we have real armies about to clash in combat and the king leads his army with a choir singing praises to The Lord. Verse 21 states that the singing went before the armed forces and while they marched towards battle, they *"kept singing."* They praised The Lord and prevailed.

The songs inspired the people to trust in God no matter what they faced. What if you and I began to lead with praise in the face of pain? Instead of complaining in agony we tune up in adulation. After all, no matter how bad things get, we know that His faithful love endures forever. Will you make up in your mind today to turn your mouth into an instrument of gratitude? Your words of praise will lead the way; it will lead you through to victory.

People who've observed your circumstance will see your faith, unwavering. Your confidence in your Lord will set the tone through your test. No matter what swords and chariots you have (natural resources), your hope isn't in them. Your trust is in your Heavenly Father to see you through. The level of victory that some circumstances require is beyond the reach of a human hand. Sometimes the victory requires supernatural intervention.

Intensify Your Praise

Verse 22 describes the intensity of the praise. This worship wasn't timid or shy, in fact it was a shout! They shouted their praises of victory and as they did the Lord brought confusion against their enemy. They celebrated the faithfulness of God with songs and because of that, their enemy went into a state of confusion. They turned on themselves and destroyed each other. Talk about sweet victory! By the time Judah arrived on the scene of the battle there were no enemies remaining, only their spoils, and so many, they couldn't even carry it all.

This is the power of praise on display. We must get in the habit of praising through the pain. No matter how bad things get, God is still good. And as we praise Him through the worst, it sets us up to see His best. Our adversary is no match for our King, so don't give up on God in death valley. Praise your way through the threats that rise against you.

It's time that we assemble in the Valley of Beracah. Let's review verse 26, noting that after they plundered their enemy for three days, the people gathered in the Valley of Beracah where they praised the Lord. Well, this word "Beracah" in Hebrew means "Praise." They named the place The Valley of Praise! They are literally giving God glory in the valley. He's that good. Even when it doesn't seem like He is, God remains good. We must trust that when life is at its worst, God is still at His best. That's real faith on display. Patiently holding on to God's promises even through pain.

Sometimes we pray for things to change. We cry out in our agony, but circumstances may worsen. Don't give up! Take your worship to another level of warfare. Encourage yourself and somebody else by proclaiming the faithfulness of His love.

The complaining that has come out of my mouth throughout the years has yielded little harvest. I haven't gotten any victory over great obstacles by whining, but when I've praised my way through pain I've come through on the other side with gains. Whether that gain was a greater level of knowing The Spirit, wisdom or healing, I got an increase. As Jehoshaphat led the people to lead with praise we'd be wise to do the same.

The Shout of Victory!

They shouted in victory after receiving the word of encouragement from The Lord. They didn't wait for the prophecy come to pass. They praised God in the face of defeat with a shout of victory. As you lay hold to the promises of God you should do the same. Promises to do us good and not to harm, and to give us a hope and a future. His promises ensure us that all things work together for the good of them who love God and are called according to His purpose. We should stand in the truth that in all things we are more than conquerors through Him that loves us. We should shout in faith that God always causes us to triumph.

Shouting may seem weird to some, but it's biblical. It's a battle cry. We've all shouted over things that were important to us, for example, a bad call at a basketball game may have sparked you to shout at the referee. Maybe your favorite team scored a point or a touchdown and you jumped and shouted. Well, in the same way, would you whisper to warn your child that danger was up ahead? No! You'd shout if they were about to walk into oncoming traffic. You'd yell at the top of your lungs to get their attention. What if you received a gift that you really wanted? You would shout at the surprise in joy. You rejoice because you are glad over the gift. Your voice becomes an extension of your emotions and your emotions react to a reality of a moment that is required."

Well, victory is taking place in our lives! We need to shout in victory. Turn the valley of shame into a valley of praise. Watch the praise unfold after the word of The Lord came to a prophet earlier in the passage we were reading above.

2 Chronicles 20:13-19 (HCSB)13

All Judah was standing before the Lord with their infants, their wives, and their children. 14 In the middle of the congregation, the Spirit of the Lord came to Jahaziel (son of Zechariah, son of Benaiah, son of Jeiel, son of Mattaniah, a Levite from Asaph's descendants), 15 and he said, "Listen carefully, all Judah and you inhabitants of Jerusalem, and King Jehoshaphat. This is what the Lord says: 'Do not be afraid or discouraged because of this vast number, for the battle is not yours, but God's. 16 Tomorrow, go down against them. You will see them coming up the Ascent of Ziz, and you will find them at the end of the valley facing the Wilderness of Jeruel. 17 You do not have to fight this battle. Position yourselves, stand still, and see the salvation of the Lord. He is with you, Judah and Jerusalem. Do not be afraid or discouraged. Tomorrow, go out to face them, for Yahweh is with you.' "

18 Then Jehoshaphat bowed with his face to the ground, and all Judah and the inhabitants of Jerusalem fell down before the Lord to worship Him. 19 Then the Levites from the sons of the Kohathites and the Korahites stood up to praise the Lord God of Israel shouting with a loud voice.

The battle that you've been claiming as yours is not, it's God's! You're facing the army, but it is God who's fighting what you're facing. The enemy seems overwhelming, but The God of The Valley won't leave you. In the word that God gave them, He told them that they didn't have to fight this battle but to just get into position. Jehoshaphat responded by falling to the ground in worship. Then, all Judah and Jerusalem worshiped in the same manner. Verse 19 says, *"The worship leaders rose up and shouted with loud voices."* Come on people of God, we've got to see this pattern. God told them to get into position to see Him win the battle for them. The position was to face their enemy with a praise on their lips and they took their stance. They shouted before, during and after the miracle.

Let's not wait until the pain subsides to give glory to God. Let's praise God while everything is going wrong, because there's power in our praise. Power to change our attitudes about what we are facing. It's the ability to magnify The Lords majesty in our hearts over the size of the pain before us. Praise will shift the atmosphere of your entire home. Fear and discouragement will melt away as you encourage yourself in the presence of The Lord. Then you will see the salvation of The Lord. Right now, today make a decision to turn your home into a valley of praise. The Valley of Beracah.

8. The Self Inflicted Valley

"Life is 10% of what happens to me and 90% of how I react to it." - John Maxwell

"Look! The Lord is coming! He leaves his throne in heaven and tramples the heights of the earth.
The mountains melt beneath his feet and flow into the valleys like wax in a fire, like water pouring down a hill."
Micah 1:3–4 (NLT)

The Lord gives this message to Micah, a prophet between 740 and 689B.C. Micah gives a prophetic message to Judah, God's people. Throughout scripture God spoke to people at various times and different ways. As for Micah, he sees a word. That sounds strange because we'd usually hear a word, but instead he sees a vision and God gives him the words to speak over the nation of Judah.

We would do well to place our ears on the Word of The Lord. To envision the written Word of God, the Bible, you and I must engage in worship of The Holy Spirit. As Jesus promised us, The Spirit would guide us into all truth. While we travel through Death Valley, we need the Light of truth. We need vision in the valley. God our Father still whispers truth to us through the Holy Spirit. Sometimes, He will cause the words of scripture to come alive. It's as if the Holy Spirit will illuminate scripture within you. Your understanding will line up to the knowledge of the truth of God's Word. What you once could not see, the Holy Spirit will enable you to understand and you'll see a word from God. You'll understand the message because God's message, amidst the madness of life, brings peace to those who'll hold to it.

This passage gives us an amazing imagery of the greatness of our God. It is one that you and I should meditate on. As Micah expounds on what he sees, he urges us to envision it with him. *"Look! The Lord is coming! Samaria and Jerusalem open your eyes and see the destruction that's coming."* This prophecy contains a word of caution about judgment upon the nation. The punishment was due to the sinfulness of the people against God. Primarily there was idolatry in the capital city. How do we know this? Verse five (5) gives us more insight:

"And why is this happening? Because of the rebellion of Israel*-- yes, the sins of the whole nation. Who is to blame for Israel's rebellion? Samaria, its capital city! Where is the center of idolatry in Judah? In Jerusalem, its capital!"

Micah 1:5 (NLT)

Some Valleys are Self-Inflicted.

Right now we live in the dispensation, or time period of grace. God welcomes all men to come to Him. He loves us unconditionally. There's forgiveness and mercy to all who come to Him in faith. There's nothing we can do to make Him love us any more or any less than what He already does. God loves people, period!

Now, with all of that being said, there's also a misconception that's rampant of our Heavenly Father. It's as if He's an angry graybeard in heaven waiting to beat or chastise His children for every mistake they make. This is a poor personification. The truth is that He's filled with grace and love. Extending mercy beyond what we ever deserve and could earn. Yet included within His love is His holiness. Scripture tells us that:

> *"Righteousness and justice are the foundation of your throne. Unfailing love and truth walk before you as attendants." Psalm 89:14 (NLT)*

There's no separating the love of the Father from His truth presiding over His children. That would be the equivalent of a parent observing and allowing their child to place their hands within a flame. This parent knows that the child will burn. The parent's love for the child compels them to protect and correct the child. This parental instinct stems from our Creator.

He's the perfect Father seated in justice and righteousness. Throughout the Old Testament we find Israel, God's chosen people, being protected and corrected. At times the judgment of The Lord can seem harsh to us, but we often fail to grasp the complete story. We missed the details of debauchery and idolatry that lead to their destruction reaped on His chosen people. In His unfailing love and truth He'd often redirect to protect and correct His people.

To this day, even under a New Testament covenant of grace and truth, The Father still corrects those He loves. Especially when we are in danger of falling into the flames of idolatry, unbelief and sin. He will love us to health. Sometimes that means allowing us to experience the consequences of our poor decisions.

No, He won't abandon us and He will never leave us because He's our Heavenly Daddy. This is a guarantee. Still, we all have moments of stubbornness, rebellion and pride. We "wave our fist in Gods face," so to speak. It's our will instead of His and we ignore the gentle, loving voice of our Lord. So, for our protection and correction, in moments like these, He gives us a glimpse of His majesty.

This valley experience may be one of our own doing. We have followed our own path and it has led us to disaster. Have you ever ignored God and found yourself in a valley? What should you do when the valley is self-inflicted?

Micah had a word for us all. He invited us to see what God was saying, so lets give it a try. God left His throne in Heaven and started to move, but where was He headed? He was going to the heights of the earth. Well, what were the highest places in the earth during Micah's time? The mountains, the mountains were. We know this because the next verse emphasizes it. *"The mountains melt beneath His feet like wax in flames..."* Can you see the imagery here?

The highest places in our world are steppingstones for Him. He skips from one slope to the next as if they were ant mounds. As the weight of God's majesty is impressed upon each mountain peak, it gets crushed under the pressure. The avalanche of the mountain is so abundant that it splits down into the valley. The valley itself ceases to exist as God levels the highest places and fills in the lowest ones! He can balance it all out as if it were nothing.

How majestic is your God? Who should we listen to in life? Whose advice should we follow by faith? Open your eyes and see, The Lord is coming. Micah spoke to a nation of people who turned away from God. It's not just that they have ignored Him; they've turned from God to worship something else. Regardless of which false god they devoted themselves to, it wasn't their loving Father.

During those times people would worship idols through ceremonies in "the high places." They'd offer sacrifices or make graven images on the high places. So, this vision spoke a powerful message stating that He will crush the idolatry and the false gods that were being worshipped in the high places! These false gods would melt like wax from the mountains to the valley.

One thing is certain God loves us all. He will protect us from anything that would harm us, even if "that thing" which causes the harm is our self. He will protect you from yourself if needed. If we have made anything our god other than Jehovah, He will protect and correct us.

"You must not make for yourself an idol of any kind or an image of anything in the heavens or on the earth or in the sea. 5 You must not bow down to them or worship them, for

I, the Lord your God, am a jealous God who will not tolerate your affection for any other gods. I lay the sins of the parents upon their children; the entire family is affected--even children in the third and fourth generations of those who reject me. 6 But I lavish unfailing love for a thousand generations on those* who love me and obey my commands."

Exodus 20:4–6 (NLT)

We see here that idolatry on the hilltop is forbidden. We also see that the sin of the parent affects the entire family. Verse five (5) makes it clear that God lays the sin of the parents on the children and their children's children.

Someone might say, "Well what does my parents sin have to do with me?" I don't deserve their judgment. That's not fair, but I would ask again that you see what's being said. For instance, lets imagine a father who's become entangled in a get rich quick scheme. Say this father is so focused on making money at all cost that he uses all his resources trying to get rich. However, let's pretend that "said scheme" doesn't pan out. Well, he looses it all. My question to you is, will his children be affected? If he can't afford life insurance will his children's children inheritance disappear? Of course! They're all affected by his greed and love of money. This man made money an idol and did whatever he could to get it. He's now pierced himself with many sorrows. Since his children are within his house, they're affected as well.

It's not that God in Heaven hates this man's children, but what God is teaching us is that our behaviors affect the community around us. Our family tree is affected by those who've come before us. Sure, we can change our family line if we've had a bad start, but that doesn't negate the fact that somehow we had rough beginnings. It was an unstable foundation from those who had gone before us.

A drug addict's behavior can send their entire family into a valley. An alcoholic's misguided priority can lead his or her family into ruin. A gambler can waste the family's future with the roll of a dice. An adulterer can break a trust and divide their entire home. A lazy woman can loose her job and fail to pay off her debts. Everyday, even God's people make boneheaded decisions that send us into valleys that are hard to get out of.

In order for us to get out of our self-inflicted valleys, we've got to repent. Now, when I first came into the church I thought repentance was turning away from sin and trying really, really hard not to do wrong again. But that definition was incomplete. The word, "repent" means to return to the original way of thinking. It's the process of having your mind renewed to the truth. There has to be a returning to the right way of believing. What you believe governs the actions you take.

In Micah's day, people believed improperly about which god was the true God. They worshipped false gods within their own minds-eye, justifiably. Now, it's easy to judge the Israelites of the Old Testament. As we read chapter after chapter of God's miraculous power, followed by Israel's rebellion, followed by God's correction and finally Israel repenting; it seems as if they were still clueless. It makes you just want to say, "why can't you guys get it right and stay right? You know how the cycle goes right?"

The truth is, these were men and women like you and I. Over time, they drifted away from the reality of their relationship with God. They'd forget about God's word and slowly conform to the culture of the communities around them. In their wealth and prosperity, they'd forget that it was God who gave it to them. After a while, they'd lose the connection with Jehovah and seek to fill it with false gods. For the sake of clarity lets call the false gods, "false hopes."

Similar to our false hopes, they fall short of the majesty of God. Drug addiction, alcoholism or porn can't satisfy. The unnecessary debt, the materialism and money won't suffice. That affair, the promiscuity and the lust fall short of satisfaction. Still, we persist down a pathway of destruction furthering ourselves down into a valley.

Mercifully, The Good Shepherd is still there with us ready and willing to provide a way of escape. Every Shepherd knows that sheep sometimes stray away, but His rod can reach out to pull us back in. His staff can comfort us in our embarrassing failures, but the real question is, will we see God in His majesty? Look, The Lord is coming and He's about to put our idols to shame to bring us back to sanity.

A beautiful statement is made in Exodus 20:6.

6. But I lavish unfailing love for a thousand generations on those who love me and obey my commands.

Those who reject Him affect their children and their third and fourth generations. But to those who'll accept Him, He lavishes unfailing love for 1000's of generations! Even under the Old Testament Covenant of law, God was more merciful than people's unrighteousness. Still to this day, there's mercy and grace in abundance to all who will turn to Him in faith.

If you've found yourself overwhelmed by the sins of your past. The consequences have piled up and you're loosing hope. Would you pray this prayer:

Heavenly Father, you are God and beside you there is no other. I will have no other God before you, including myself. I am sorry for ignoring your voice. I ask for your forgiveness of all my sins. I receive your love, your grace and your mercy today. I believe that you love me and you have never left me. I accept your grace and forgiveness. I ask that you would fill me with your Holy Spirit. Guide me into all truth. Help me to see you in your majesty. Help me to overcome and to move forward in life. Give me peace that passes all understanding. In Jesus name, I thank you for forgiveness and a new start. Amen.

9. The Valley of God

"We all want Canaan without going through the wilderness." - Ravi Zacharias

You are the fruition of God's design and creativity. You aren't a random chance. Somewhere within the genius of God's mind, within His amazing artistic imagination He created you. You're a reflection of Him to the world and to the universe for that matter. You indeed are the intentionality of God's own free will. You are His choice and your life matters. You are the apple of His eye. In other words, God can't open His eyes without seeing you within His scope of vision.

I want to encourage you to cry out to God in your moments of doubt or despair. Know this, He can see and hear you and He can respond to rescue you. You matter to God. And your life with all its complexities has meaning within His eternal masterpiece. Though you may not see the full scope of the reasoning behind what God allows within your life, trust that at the end the story there is a win.

"I am praying to you because I know you will answer, O God. Bend down and listen as I pray. Show me your unfailing love in wonderful ways. By your mighty power you rescue those who seek refuge from their enemies. Guard me as you would guard your own eyes. Hide me in the shadow of your wings."
Psalm 17:6–8 (NLT)

Is it possible with the evil that is against us, fighting us, God can reveal His love through and to us? As God listens and bows down into the affairs of men, we see His holy hands and mighty power. He rescues the afflicted from their captors. From the calamity in your life, God can take the fragments of brokenness and weave together a beautiful tapestry. Have you ever looked back on your life and remembered a crisis and knew the only way you could've made it through was with the loving hand of God? I pose a question then, could we have experienced that level of awe and insight into His majesty over the madness without going through the mess?

Why is this essential you might ask? Well, there are moments when we don't understand the dark days within God's sovereign plan. Although I do not believe that God is the cause of evil, I do know that He can see it before it arrives at the doorstep. Before anything happens to us, God in His omniscience can see it coming. At times, this is hard to process. This leaves me thinking, "you could've prevented this! Why did you allow this to happen?"

The horrors that happen within humanity can cause us to question our connection to our Creator. It may cause us to question His intent for our lives or the extent of His involvement. Some valleys can flow deep within two high mountain ranges and in doing so, block out the sunlight. It can get so dark that we wonder if the light even exists anymore. Please my brother, my sister, know this...there's a Great God, your Creator who's walking with you and His plan will prevail. I urge you pray that Psalm until the shadows of death are replaced with the comfort of the shadow of His wings.

The God of the Valley

He is literally called, *"The God of Valley"* in scripture. The passage that we are about to read takes place as the Israelites are on their exodus from Egypt. They're headed to their promised land called Canaan. God leads Moses to take His chosen people, Israel through a journey in a wilderness prior to the promise land. Sounds fun right? Of course not! Especially when we learn in scripture that there was a short cut to Canaan that

God knew about. When Pharaoh let the people go, they could've headed down a different route, but God knew they weren't ready to handle possessing the promise. So He sends them on a journey to protect and perfect them.

God is patient. God knows what we need to succeed. He can see the future and how to protect us and perfect us, even though we don't quite understand what in the world He's doing sometimes. Israel went on this long journey of believing God and then doubting God. Believing God and then doubting God again and every time they began to doubt, God would work a miracle to prove His trustworthiness. This would sooth their doubts temporarily. Then, at the next site of struggle, at the very next "valley" they'd walk through, He'd have to prove Himself all over again. Does this sound familiar to anyone reading this?

"From there the Israelites traveled to Beer, which is the well where the Lord said to Moses, 'Assemble the people, and I will give them water.' There the Israelites sang this song:

'Spring up, O well! Yes, sing its praises! Sing of this well, which princes dug, which great leaders hollowed out with their scepters and staffs.' Then the Israelites left the wilderness and proceeded on through Mattanah, Nahaliel, and Bamoth. After that they went to the valley in Moab where Pisgah Peak overlooks the wasteland."
Numbers 21:16–20 (NLT)

For some of you, while reading that passage you rejoiced because you saw the word "Beer" in the Bible, but what this word translates into is something quite different. It represents one of those places where the people complained again. God then shows His capability to carry them and His care for His children. They needed a drink and God gave them a well in the wilderness! You see, they created a worship song from the situation! Some of us could make melodies worth singing from some of the situations in which God has saved us. We've all got a Beer on the inside, springing up from the miracle working provision of God! Where's your journal? Where's your song? It would be wise to write what you've witnessed in the wilderness so that you can recite the miraculous moments that God has performed in your life. When the darkness seeks to sink you into despair you can worship your way into the light.

After they worshipped over the provisions of God, they proceeded to the promise land. Before moving forward to my main point, I pray you receive this: don't stop moving forward to your promise land. Your life is so meaningful, too meaningful to allow it to go to waste in trepidation and insecurity. Who you are and whose you are must resonate throughout every part of your being! You are the apple of God's eye. One translation of that statement is that you are the little man in His eye. You are essentially God's "Mini Me", His child, and never forget that. Proceed through where you were to get to where you're going, the promise land.

Along this journey, Israel would set up camp at different cities or build encampments. One of those campsites was called Nahaliel. Nahaliel in the Hebrew language means: Valley of God. This place is recorded here for a purpose. It allows us to backtrack the journey of God's chosen people on their way to the Promised Land. This is the history of Judaism and Christianity. However there's little mentioned outside of this verse about this place. Very little to draw from other than a general region in which they setup an encampment.

What if in our personal pathways of life we viewed God's sovereignty as unlimited? The sovereignty of God is His absolute right to do all things according to His own good pleasure. God is not only involved on the mountaintops of life, but also in the valleys. Although He might not be the cause of the chaos, He can still control the crisis. He indeed is our God of the valley! The mountains that create the shadows looming over us melt at the awesome wonder of who created them!

"The mountains melt like wax before the Lord, before the Lord of all the earth."

Psalm 97:5 (NLT)

He's Not Limited in His Lordship.

He reigns as King over all things and this includes the valley. What does this mean for us? It means that the purposes and plans for our lives in which God has prepared it, will prevail! You may not understand why you're there right now or how long you'll be there, but just know, this season will not be in vain. He's equipping you for where He's taking you.

"The Lord frustrates the plans of the nations and thwarts all their schemes. But the Lord's plans stand firm forever; his intentions can never be shaken. What joy for the nation whose God is the Lord, whose people he has chosen as his inheritance. The Lord looks down from heaven and sees the whole human race. From his throne he observes all who live on the earth. He made their hearts, so he understands everything they do." Psalm 33:10–15

"But the Lord watches over those who fear him, those who rely on his unfailing love. He rescues them from death and

keeps them alive in times of famine. We put our hope in the Lord. He is our help and our shield. In him our hearts rejoice, for we trust in his holy name."
Psalm 33:18-21 (NLT)

I don't know what schemes our adversary has plotted against you, but I do know that God will frustrate his plans. God's plan for your life will stand firm forever and He won't be shaken. Will you trust in Him today as He looks down from His throne over your situation? Reverence Him, not as some distant and uncaring entity, but as One who has unfailing love for you. The One who made your heart and watches over you. Put your hope in the Lord again. Trust God again on the basis of His sovereignty. Know that He can transform tragedy to triumph at any moment in time.

Put your hope in the Lord. His name is holy. Holy means sanctifying or cleansing. Allow the credibility of God's holiness to wash away the stench of doubt and fear. The Lord is your Shepherd and He reigns over the valley that He's walking you through. Rely on His unfailing love. Lean on it and cleave to it. Let God's unconditional love be the support for your hurting heart in difficult times.

> *"The Lord of Heaven's Armies has sworn this oath:*
> *It will all happen as I have planned.*
> *It will be as I have decided."*
> Isaiah 14:24 (NLT)

How Did We Get to Suffering?

Going back to the fall of man with Adam and Eve, God created a perfect world. He was expressing His love for humanity through His creative glory. But in this majestic paradise where God's presence dwelt with them in the garden, He allowed Satan to slither his way in. Why? What in world was Satan doing there in the paradise of God's plan? Some may wonder why even place the tree of the Knowledge of Good and Evil in the garden only to tell them not to eat from it. The fall of man could've been prevented right? Sure, it could've been prevented. The question that we may need to ask is... should it have been prevented? Could it be that Satan, the serpent, and the tree within the Garden was part of the plan and purpose of God? I believe that it was all part of a bigger plan than what mankind could understand at that time. Despite the fact that God gave them warning before their destruction, they still made the wrong choice. It changed the course of mankind, but it didn't change God's predestined plan and purpose.

Within God's omniscience, His all-knowingness, He makes plans with victory in mind. And though the choices of mankind change, His perfect plan prevails. He doesn't change and neither does His will. He's prepared for the future because of His foreknowledge. His agenda is unstoppable because His foreknowledge accounts for every variable.

Paul writes in Ephesians that God's plan was to upgrade mankind from His creation to His children. From the beginning He knew this would happen but it didn't make sense to mankind until Christ fulfilled the saving work of the cross.

"Praise the God and Father of our Lord Jesus Christ, who has blessed us in Christ with every spiritual blessing in the heavens. For He chose us in Him, before the foundation of the world, to be holy and blameless in His sight. In love He predestined us to be adopted through Jesus Christ for Himself, according to His favor and will, to the praise of His glorious grace that He favored us with in the Beloved. We have redemption in Him through His blood, the forgiveness of our trespasses, according to the riches of His grace that He lavished on us with all wisdom and understanding. He made known to us the mystery of His will, according to His good pleasure that He planned in Him for the administration of the days of fulfillment, to bring everything together in the Messiah, both things in heaven and things on earth in Him."
Ephesians 1:3–10 (HCSB)

This passage could be a book in itself, but what I hope to reveal in this is what Paul calls a mystery. Before the world was even created, God wanted mankind, who He knew would become sinful, to be holy. He wanted sinful men who deserved His judgement and punishment to be blameless. In love, He predestined us to adoption. His plan was to combine celestial things with terrestrial things. His creation of flesh and blood to become one body covered by his Heavenly blood!

This is mind-blowing foresight and purposefulness. This is infinite wisdom at work. Throughout human history, God was weaving together the story of redemption. From the very first tragic decision of Adam and Eve God was graciously preparing humanity for the Promised Land! Did He cause the fall? No, but He did use it to His glory. He recycled the mess with a mystery. Adam and Eve didn't know God's big idea and Satan didn't know what God was up to within humanity. Right now in your life you may not know what God is up to or what victory will come through the suffering that you're facing right now, but God's loving plan will prevail.

In the end we always win. God always causes us to triumph and His will works all things together. You may not be able to make sense of the pains of the past yet, but know that God can take what was meant for evil against you and make it work together for good.

For humanity, we'd have no song of redemption without the suffering. Even if we sung a song of redemption we wouldn't appreciate the words because we wouldn't understand the reality HIs love, mercy, favor and grace.

So Sean, are you implying that God caused the evil? Absolutely not! First of all, Satan and the Kingdom of darkness are the causes of evil. Second, we must understand that Satan is not God's equal. He is evil, a liar, the embodiment of hate and he causes death. God is holy, loving and is the Author of life. Within creation, it was necessary that the garden had Satan and the trees within it. In order for mankind to truly have the freedom of choice, there had to be options to choose. Why? Well in order to truly love someone, it must be of that person's free will. How can one choose to love someone if they've never been given the choice not to love them? You see, within the perfect plan of God mankind would be free will moral agents able to choose their place within His destined plan. By design, from His love He offers us a relationship with Himself. He gives us life and love and with that comes the opportunity to reject him. God's perfect plan was that man would have choice on His earth, within His sovereignty.

When we reflect on this mystery, we find no point within time that our Eternal God has been defeated. He's in control of all things. He is perfect and His will is perfect, even though the things created within His will contain imperfections. When mankind fell by following the advice of Satan, was this God's will? No, it wasn't! God doesn't cause the evil, but He does foresee it. With God's foreknowledge of the fall, He creates a plan to redeem His creation. His eternal solution was to suffer as our substitution through the cross of Calvary. He enters into our suffering and becomes our Savior to His own glory. Jesus was sent to this earth to accomplish a purpose that only He could fulfill, The Cross of our redemption!

God's choice was to not allow our poor choices to destroy us all. He steps into our brokenness to break the bondage of sin and grants us an eternal win. His plan before the world began was through His love, He'd enter into the valley of suffering to rescue those that were stuck in sin, that they'd be redeemed through Him.

I'm quite sure Jesus didn't like the pain of the cross. It wasn't easy to bear, but after the resurrection He knew it would be worth it. Know this, what you've had to endure may have cost you years of embarrassment, tears of frustration and nights of sleeplessness. You may have had your days of anger and moments where you felt like giving up. Jesus bore the same pain that your journey has endured and He overcame that so you would overcome. You are not alone on your journey; Jesus meets you right there to carry you through until He makes all things new.

"So then, since we have a great High Priest who has entered heaven, Jesus the Son of God, let us hold firmly to what we believe. This High Priest of ours understands our weaknesses, for he faced all of the same testing's we do, yet he did not sin. So let us come boldly to the throne of our gracious God. There we will receive his mercy, and we will find grace to help us when we need it most."

Hebrews 4:14–16 (NLT)

I'm persuaded that Satan wants to try his best to drive a wedge between you and the One who can help you most. He will do so by trying to get you to believe that God is the One who's punishing you, as if God has abandoned you. Satan will lie and whisper that God doesn't exist, or you deserve what you're going through. These are all lies! Please run to the presence of the One who walked in the shoes of your suffering. In fact, you should come boldly! Tell Him how you feel, cast your cares on Him and receive grace to help you in your hour of need. He understands what it's like to face the pain of abandonment. Jesus knows what its like to face rejection and abandonment by those closest to Him. So run into His presence to experience His comfort and peace. Talk with God about whatever you feel. Write out what's on your heart and speak with Him about it. During your time in worship you'll experience a comfort unlike anything that we can find in this world.

10. Just Keep Walking

"At your greatest point of suffering, in your greatest time of need; by your side you will find Him and forever He will be...The God of the Valley." - Sean Reed

*"The Lord is my shepherd; I shall not want.
Even though I walk through the valley of the shadow of death, I will fear no evil, for you are with me; your rod and your staff, they comfort me."
Psalm 23:1; 4 (ESV)*

A valley is a low area between hills and mountains. A shadow is defined as a dark area or shape produced by a body coming between light rays and a surface. Death is the personification of the power that destroys life. David in our times may have said it this way, even though I'm walking in Death Valley I will not fear for my life.

When we're startled by something we tend to jump back. Shrinking away from the threat in defense mode. It's our protective instinct to avoid pain. At all cost we want to preserve life so we back away from death. Imagine a giant spider sitting outside of your bedroom door in the morning. You turn on the light and catch a glimpse of this tarantula and chills shoot throughout your body. What would you do?

Picture a car driving erratically towards your family and you react in fear to the danger. Your pulse starts racing and out of instinct you tense up as you evade danger. There's nothing wrong with that at all, it's your natural instinct kicking in for survival.

Do you also have a similar response to threats in the valley? It's not healthy for us to live a life on edge of fearing the worst and never enjoying the rest; wasting entire seasons of life under stress and fear and gripping our hearts day in and day out. Worry can choke the life out of you. Sure we can pray, go to church and do all the things that Christians should yet we're still so stressed and overwhelmed in these difficult seasons.

I've come to realize that the shadows of death can become a greater reality than the Shepherd walking by our side in the valley. If we aren't careful we can pray to the God of life about the shadows of death out of fear instead of faith. Essentially believing the threat is greater than the One who created the valley itself.

Living in the Face of Death

David put to pen some of the greatest words ever written. Within this Psalm he establishes an order of priority and power. Priority in that he didn't lead off the writing with the antagonist of the story. Instead he starts with The Author of the story itself. The Lord is my Shepherd.

"My Shepherd," implies that David views God as his personal guide and in the same breath reveals that he is in fact God's sheep. We are if we so choose to believe it, God's property, which makes us God's responsibility. If we are talking about entrusting our lives to a random shepherd there'd be cause for concern, but Jesus said the Good Shepherd would go so far to provide for the sheep... and He'd lay down His very life for them!

If we let that sink in, it's amazing. It also makes sense then to continue walking in Death Valley. For whenever a sheep needs life, Jesus reminds us that He's already laid it down for us. Right where we can get it, there's resurrection power that abides within us everyday so we don't have to want for anything. We know that everything needed is in the One who's walking beside us.

Could it be that someone has threatened you and you can't stop thinking about it? The trauma of a family crisis may be weighing heavily on your heart. Is there a moment of financial tension that has your mind stressing out? Lets call that a financial death valley. I want to encourage you today to keep walking. Take it one day and one step at a time with God, in faith. Determine within yourself that you will not fear evil. After all, no one has ever been killed by a shadow! Our adversary, the evil one, is a deceiver and an imposter. He masquerades himself as a glorious angel when in fact he's a defeated foe because Jesus crushed him with the cross. Life has already conquered death and life will always dispel the darkness.

On your way towards the exit of your valley, know that it is well with your soul because your soul has a personal overseer. The rod and staff of God will be His personal weaponry against the evil adversaries that lurk within the darkness. Persevere through the insinuations of hopelessness and the whispers of worry. Rejoice in advance in The Shepherd who always causes you to triumph.

Imagine for a moment that you're in a movie theater. A friend invited you and so you gladly accepted the invite but you aren't privy to what the film is all about. You pick up your popcorn and snacks, grab your favorite seats, proceed to chat through the previews and finally wait for the movie to start. Quickly you realize that this is a horror film. At one point in the movie you brace yourself because you know what's coming. The main character heads towards an exit but they have to find out what the noise was on the other side of the door. As they turn the doorknob everyone knows that something frightening is lurking on the other side. Sooner or later the scary music will blaze and the predator jumps out and threatens the life of the person.

Let me ask you something, whether you're the "hardened scary movie fan" or the "I hate horror films" person...did you jump? At some point, if the film is scary enough, we will still jump. Even though we know these are actors, there are cameras all around, it's not real blood its only makeup and this is all fiction, still we jump out of fear. The fear of something that isn't real.

This is what it looks like when we are afraid of the shadows. We jump at the illusion of spiritual danger, financial ruin or the loss of a relationship. Could it be that we stop walking in faith because we begin to marvel at the size of the shadow? Think this through... We've all taken a flashlight and made bunny ears on the wall or an alligator shadow on the side of the tent. Yes, there's a real hand, there's a real flashlight, and there's the appearance of an alligator or bunny rabbit. But everyone knows those shadows aren't real. So there's no need to be afraid.

Just as the hand is smaller than the image it cast, the kingdom of darkness puffs itself up as well. It brags and boasts on how much damage has been or will be done and they try to cast a great shadow of death. Where you and I must begin to agree with David is in the truth.

The truth that there can be no shadow seen unless a light is behind the hand! There's a great light that shines from the throne of God and you are never alone and have no need to be afraid.

Yes, there's a real hand. That may be a negative doctors report. Sure, there's trouble in some relationships. The hand may be the fact that you've been laid off. Maybe people have turned their backs on you. These are real things just like the hand, but have you gotten so focused on the horror in the film that you forget it's all scripted? God is The Author of your life story and He's greater than every character in the story that He wrote. And yet, He chooses to costar in the film of your life. You must choose to keep walking no matter what because this scene isn't the end of your story.

"The Lord directs the steps of the godly. He delights in every detail of their lives. Though they stumble, they will never fall, for the Lord holds them by the hand. Once I was young, and now I am old.

Yet I have never seen the godly abandoned or their children begging for bread."
Psalm 37:23–25 (NLT)

The last scene of your life may have startled you to the point that you didn't think you'd make it. You've felt as though it's too difficult to bounce back. You've stumbled, but you haven't fallen. God's got your hand right now. You are not alone. He will supply your needs and even provide some wants! Look back over your life for a moment and meditate on how you've made it through; our Heavenly Father will not abandon His people. Just keep walking my friends.

When you can't quite see your way through the shadows of death, continue to talk to the God of life. He delights in every detail of your life. Talk to Him about everything instead of dwelling on your problems. Speak the Truth about how good your Father is when life is at its worst. Paul the Apostle told us:

"For we walk by faith, not by sight."
2 Corinthians 5:7 (ESV)

If you go by what you see in the natural realm, deception is inevitable and if you're anything like me then your body language changes. Your demeanor gets all tensed up, attitudes become all stressed out and your mind isn't at peace because it's racing through all the myriad of possibilities. Get a grip on yourself! Take it one step of faith at a time. Open your mouth and declare, "Lord, you are my Shepherd!" Go into a place of worship from a place of victory instead of victimization. Praise God because it's well with your soul, because there's a well of life flowing in your soul. Death can't quench it and Satan can't take your joy when you're in this place of faith and worship. Your Heavenly Father will beat back the enemy and bring you sweet rest.

11. Anoint My Head With Oil

"You prepare a feast for me in the presence of my enemies. You honor me by anointing my head with oil. My cup overflows with blessings.
Surely your goodness and unfailing love will pursue me all the days of my life, and I will live in the house of the Lord forever."
Psalm 23:5–6 (NLT)

David introduced us to a myriad of benefits from The Shepherd. God is preparing a table of food and drink for us. Can you picture your Heavenly Father making a feast for you? Well He's throwing down and that's a blessing because I love food! It's my nourishment. It gives me comfort and of course keeps me alive. Chef Jesus is preparing a spread of nourishment just for you, right in front of your enemies no less. That makes the meal all the more special.

Right there in the valley God is cooking up a meal for your benefit. He does it right in the presence of those who are attempting to take your life. His hands carefully provide the feast for your benefit. The table placed in front of you has food already prepared, so much food and blessings that your cup is running over!

Every child of God should believe that He would supply all your needs. From His own personal stash of wealth and abundance He will supply the full dose, both for our bodies, our souls, the life that we're living on this earth and the life that is to come. God cares for you, His sheep. So much so that The Shepherd becomes the host of a feast thrown on behalf of His sheep at His own expense.

Every day of our lives we can pray that God supplies our daily bread, but we need to pray in faith and believe that what we've asked Him for when we've prayed will come.

It would do us well to eliminate all forms of worry in the valley. For every thought of worry is a waste of time. We can't add one cent to our bank accounts by worrying. The promotion won't come through stressing over it. The application won't process faster by thinking about it all night. No, we must trust in The God of the valley.

If I was your enemy and I wanted to take you out, I'd try to get into your head, but not in an overt or obvious kind of way. I'd be crafty and subtle in my approach. In fact, I'd rather you not even know the whispers of worry were coming from me. Satan is a manipulator who masquerades as an angel of light. He's deceived even the very elect the Bible says. How does he deceive people? How can he deceive some of the best of us? After all no one wants to wake up and worry about relationships, finance or their future, but still it happens. Believers don't typically go looking for a reason to be offended and yet many have become offended and wounded in relationships.

What's Going on in The Valley?

Well, verse five (5) is packing the answer to our problem. As we go back to David's origins, before becoming the king of Israel, he was a shepherd to sheep. He wrote this passage from a personal perspective. He walked in the shoes of a shepherd tending to sheep. His experience gives valuable insight to the benefits of a loving shepherd guiding sheep.

David sheds light on the benevolence of our Heavenly Father. God's willingness to provide generously our spiritual and physical nourishment is evident. There's even an honor placed on the head of the sheep. It's done through the anointing of the sheep's head with oil.

Why is this the answer to the problem of worry, fear, bitterness or depression? I could name all manner of problems believers encounter in the valley of the shadow of death. What you'll find in common with said "problems" is that they begin in the heart or mind. Worry, fear, anxiety, depression and bitterness are all within our emotions and thoughts. They aren't physical forces but they are spiritual forces. Panic attacks or stress-induced headaches are outward signs of inward distress. The panic and stress originate in the spiritual realm.

Well Sean, what does that have to do with the sheep? David is pointing to a shepherd anointing the head of sheep. In doing so, he honors his children at a feast. It's an action that has both physical and spiritual truths.

You see, shepherds were familiar with climate changes and how these changes effected the environment. During the warmer seasons there would be great clouds of flies, mosquitos and insects that would swarm the flock. Some sheep-men even call the summer time fly time. During this time some sheep would contract nasal bot flies. Other sheep-men call them nose flies. These insects would try to burrow their way into their nasal and ear passageways. If these flies were successful at entering into these passageways, the summer could turn dreadful. In some cases it could even turn deadly for the sheep. When they get inside they buzz within the sheep's head trying to deposit their eggs on the mucous membranes of the sheep's nose. If they accomplish that, the eggs will hatch and begin to form small larvae. As you can image the larvae makes their way up into the sheep's head and causes tremendous irritation and inflammation. To relieve themselves of this irritation the sheep will hit their heads against objects to try to stop the pain. They may loose their sight due to infection; others will randomly sprint away from the flock and or drop in exhaustion from their attempts at eluding the flies. Some sheep have even killed themselves after running headfirst into trees or rocks.

The solution to fly time is for the shepherd to rub the head of the sheep with a special oil mixture. It was a mixture of special spices and olive oil. This mixture was rubbed around the nose, ears and throughout the body to detract the flies from entry. David called this anointing his head with oil in the presence of his enemy! Believers are not only given provision from God, but also protection from predators.

Ironically there's an alternative name given to Satan. It is Baalzebub, meaning Lord of the flies. Essentially calling him the prince of demons. Demons throughout the New Testament sought to occupy and torment people. I know this may sound weird to some, but it's a spiritual reality.

Regardless that this may make us uncomfortable, there's truth in it. Demons are disembodied spirits that seek to attack our minds with lies. Lies about God to us, lies about ourselves and even to those around us. Similar to the nose fly, these demons seek an opportunity to embed lies within us. If these lies about God, ourselves or other people are embedded within our minds, they'll grow. Over time they will become tormenting larvae that cause infection. This infection, as with the sheep, may lead to spiritual blindness. This is a loss of vision in life. Losing sight of God's presence in the shadows of darkness. It's the inability to see the truth about the kingdom of darkness and its schemes against us. A word from the enemy, if unchecked at the ear or eye gate of our souls, could lead to entire seasons of frustration and we the sheep will seek to ease the pain physically. All the while the solution is to rid ourselves of the spiritual impregnation within.

To avoid the summer of torture, shepherd's would anoint them with the oil to protect them from the pestilence. Well what does this look like for you and I? How do we get this oil of protection? Let's begin with a journey into where the oil comes from. The oil used for anointing the sheep was from the olive tree. In order for the oil extraction to happen it had to be crushed. Where there was no crushing of the olive, there was no extracting of the oil.

Good thing for us that Jesus chose to become our Good Shepherd. He would lay down His life for His sheep. Now, as Jesus is readying Himself for crucifixion, He spends some time in prayer. He frequently prayed at a particular place called The Garden of Gethsemane. Let's read this passage of scripture.

> "Then Jesus went with them to the olive grove called Gethsemane, and he said,
> 'Sit here while I go over there to pray.'"
> Matthew 26:36–42 (NLT)

There are items that correspond to the words of Psalm 23 and this passage. One is the olive grove found within Gethsemane. Let's discuss the olive grove. The name Gethsemane translates as the olive press. Jesus is praying in the place of the pressing or crushing. This is where the oil gets extracted for the heads of His sheep.

Our oil flows from the Shepherd Himself. While Jesus was with His disciples He told them that it was for their benefit that He died. If Jesus wasn't crucified and if He didn't rise from the dead, the Holy Spirit couldn't come. The oil is symbolic of the Holy Spirit! The Spirit of The Lord lives inside of the believer; He's our protector, He guides us into all truth. (See John 16:13) The Holy Spirit is the One who anoints our heads with the Truth about God, ourselves and other people around us.

This is the ultimate protection from the predator's infectious ways. Trusting in the truth that the Holy Spirit leads us is critical to warding off falsehoods. I've never seen worry, fear, depression or hate, yet I've believed things that weren't true that led me to embrace these unhealthy ways of thinking. I've had moments where I was consumed with palpable fear or anxiety. Having lived through the swarms of flies that came upon me, I can honestly say that the fear and anxiety may have been based on facts, but not the Truth.

There is a difference between truth and fact! Facts can change, but truth is everlasting. For instance, when I was growing up Pluto was a planet. If I would've answered on a test that there was one less planet in the solar system than the facts, as we understood them then, I would've been wrong. But now, all of a sudden with better lenses and telescopes we know that the facts were wrong. The truth is that Pluto isn't all that we thought it to be. Boy was my teachers and the entire scientific community wrong.

Can we be just as wrong about God abandoning us in the Valley of the Shadow of Death? Maybe He's right there with you. What if the provision that we think isn't coming based on the facts, is in actuality coming right out of the oven as we speak? Could it be that we've been wrong about an entire season of suffering? We're listening to the twisted whispers buzzing through our ears from Beelzebub and doubts are creeping in.

We need fresh oil on our heads today. We'd be wise to spend time in the presence of God, worshipping our Father with gladness in the truth. Instead of running to God in response of the lies, we should approach Him with trust. There should be confidence from the sheep in the love and care of our Good Shepherd. Even when we don't understand why circumstances have taken a turn for the worst, we know that God is still at His best. Get into the Bible's truth about God. Spend time reciting His promises of provision and protection then worship Him in Spirit and truth.

The Oil of Gladness

Oil in the Bible tradition was symbolic of joy and gladness. One-way of saying Ps. 23:5 is "You anoint my head with the oil of gladness." Joy isn't merely the laughter that accompanies a great joke; joy is a powerful force. To have joy means that you have the ability to rejoice as one who knows they possess victory. What a powerful person you are when you can wake up no matter what you're facing with the will to rejoice. Imagine if you possessed the ability to worship through the worst that life can throw at you. Not as a victim desperate to get a blessing, but as a victorious believer who praises despite a perceived loss. That my friend is joy!

Now, as we look back at the Psalm, it makes sense that one can sit in the presence of their enemy with a feast spread. This person that's at the table is rejoicing because the feast of The Lord is going on. They recognize the blessing of being the honored guest. This person realizes that they're blessed beyond the enemy's ability to take it away. That is a victorious person with real joy. Do you want to have this kind of anointing on your life? Well, it's available to you through a relationship with the person of the Holy Spirit.

You might be at a point in your marriage where the facts say that there's no hope. The flies are buzzing divorce. In that moment you have to escape into worship and the Word of God. You need the fresh oil of joy applied to your mind and heart. Find yourself speaking the truth and pressing through the darkness of the valley.

Do this constantly! Not as a one time 'maybe this will work' thing, but as a lifestyle. Especially after you've already been infected by a lie, at that point you'll have to not only clear out the surface lies, but also those larvae that have traveled up to your mind.

There may be a season on your job where it seems too toxic an environment to stay. You may feel overwhelmed by an incident that keeps happening. Maybe the boss is a thorn in your side. Instead of jumping to conclusions of what to do, spend time with the Holy Spirit and get the truth. You never know, God may soon remove the person you're running from to give you their position. He may be teaching you something valuable for your future through this trial. If you run from it, you'll run right back into it the next place you land until you learn from it. Could the facts be misleading you?

To this day there are cultures that embrace the anointing of the head with oil. In the Bible days it was a common practice for the host of the home to anoint their guest. Jesus was at the home of a Pharisee meeting with a group of religious leaders. Then a woman comes into the room to worship Jesus. As she did this the host of the home became distraught over Jesus allowing such a woman to touch him. Jesus responds to them in a powerful way:

"Then turning toward the woman he said to Simon, 'Do you see this woman? I entered your house; you gave me no water for my feet, but she has wet my feet with her tears and wiped them with her hair. You gave me no kiss, but from the time I came in she has not ceased to kiss my feet. You did not anoint my head with oil, but she has anointed my feet with ointment.'" Luke 7:44-46

Notice that Jesus said that you did not anoint my "head" with oil. This was the common custom of the culture. From this passage we see that other parts of a persons body could be covered as well. This is powerful in that it reveals that not only can the Holy Spirit guard our minds, but our entire being.

"It is like fine oil on the head, running down on the beard, running down Aaron's beard onto his robes." Psalm 133:2 (HCSB)

This passage is referring to the practice of qualifying a person for serving God as a priest. A person couldn't elect himself or herself for priestly service with God. They had to be chosen by God and then anointed or set apart. They were singled out as special. The person called out by God for a specific purpose. You and I are His people and we are a royal priesthood.

"But you are a chosen race, a royal priesthood, a holy nation, a people for his own possession, that you may proclaim the excellencies of him who called you out of darkness into his marvelous light. Once you were not a people, but now you are God's people; once you had not received mercy, but now you have received mercy."
1 Peter 2:9–10 (ESV)

Once we were disconnected from God, we didn't have His Spirit living within us. The darkness was our domain. The flies were accepted as the norm, but no more. We are a people of victory and praise. For God has brought us out from that dark place underneath the tyranny of Baalzebub and now we are God's people and the sheep of His pasture! It's a new day with fresh oil. We are His own possession and His anointed priesthood.

As you set yourself in the presence of God the times of refreshing are renewed. Worry, fear, depression and bitterness have to bow to the presence of your King. There's only one God in the valley and Jehovah is His name.

Some of us are praying that God remove the problem that He drives out the enemy. But isn't it more impressive if you have victory in the face of the one trying to take you out? Despite impending danger God will provide for you and your cup will overflow. In light of this truth, we must learn to be joyful even if the worst swarm of flies encroaches upon us. One of my favorite passages is Psalm 91.Take a moment to read it.

As you worship and engage in communion with the Holy Spirit, you slip into His shelter. All the benefits of this passage are at the disposal of the one who seeks the safety of God's presence. Will you engage in worship of the Holy Spirit today? Instead of following your physical inclinations or any unhealthy emotions, make a habit of seeking the shelter of the Most High God.

12. Your Cup is Running Over

"Even when I walk through the darkest valley,
I will not be afraid, for you are close beside me.
Your rod and your staff protect and comfort me.
You prepare a feast for me in the presence of my enemies.
You honor me by anointing my head with oil. My cup
overflows with blessings."
Psalm 23:4–5 (NLT)

David expresses here that we become the guest of God, the host. Similar to the disciples with Jesus at the last supper before Jesus' crucifixion, we dine with Jesus. And ironically His enemy was at the supper as well. The Bible says that Satan entered into Judas as he determined in his heart to betray Jesus. Still, Jesus kissed him. Talk about being cool under pressure!

The psalmist gives us the imagery of a cup running over, meaning there's more than enough meat and drink at the Lord's table for His honored guests. But where's this table set? It's set in the setting of the valley of the shadow of death. Contrary to my natural tendency to escape pain through fight or flight, there's a grace for the guest here. God's not provoking us to exit quickly, but rather to feast confidently at His own graciousness.

Like the Hebrew boys in the Babylonian furnace, God doesn't blow out the fire but rather enables them to endure the flames. What courageous faith! To face the flames boldly and confident that God is able to deliver whether He does or not.

This is the mindset that we must posses in times of suffering, pain or tribulation in life. God can deliver me, but regardless to when, I'll feast on His goodness for He is with me.

This Psalm begins as a picture of a shepherd caring for sheep. Then it becomes a portrait of the King graciously pouring out rich provision on His guests. He's the host to those who'll sit down and rest at His table. These children of our Heavenly Father have more faith in Him than their adversary. Somehow they find satisfaction in the abundant provisions from above. These are both spiritual and physical blessings of provision sent from Heaven. You can live with contentment in whatever state of life that we find ourselves in.

The Table is Spread

Verse five (5) emphasizes a cup of blessing running over, so there's got to be a saucer lying around somewhere! He's not a God of waste but of purpose. If there's an overflow in your cup, could it be that you'll be able to share with those around you? The cup runs over with joy, peace, patience and love so that those around us in lack can experience God through our overflow. You see, there's someone around you in need, and to whom much is given, much is required. When God gives you overflow, know that it's to share with your friends and loved ones too.

Well Sean, you just don't understand. I wish I had overflow right now. I don't have a "running over", I have barely enough and I'm in so much pain right now. What about the suffering that my loved ones are going through? There are a lot of dark nights filled with tears and it seems that bad things continue to pile up. What am I supposed to do?

Take comfort in knowing that Jesus sympathizes and empathizes with our pain. To sympathize is to take pity, to feel sorry for what someone is going through, but God does more than this. He empathizes with us, which is to feel the pain with us. Sympathy looks on someone's pain and feels sorry for them, but you can't truly relate to what they're going through. Empathy is to walk in the shoes of someone and struggle with them. This is vital to our faith. If you believe that God can't feel your pain, that He's not empathetic to your situation, would you rely on Him in your time of tribulation?

It's also difficult to cast your cares on the One whom you believe to be the source of your affliction. If you think that He's punishing you in some way for what you've done, then He's in cahoots with your demise and He wills your destruction. Would you put your life in His hands? It's hard to place your faith in Him if you don't trust in His love. Worst is if you're actually afraid of Him.

I repeat, He feels your pain and He has compassion for you, but how can we be sure of this? Scripture makes this clear.

"This High Priest of ours understands our weaknesses, for he faced all of the same testing's we do, yet he did not sin. 16 So let us come boldly to the throne of our gracious God. There we will receive his mercy, and we will find grace to help us when we need it most."
Hebrews 4:15–16 (NLT)

Jesus our High Priest understands the same testing's that we endure. He knows rejection, affliction, abandonment and physical pain. Jesus experienced grief over His city and the loss of loved ones. He walked in this world as God in human flesh. He experienced the depravity, trauma and the frailty of the human condition. Jesus, your Heavenly representative before the Fathers throne, feels your pain, so go boldly in prayer to your Heavenly Father. You have a representative in Heaven at the throne of God interceding for you in your weakest moments. No, He's not immune to our suffering because He walked in our shoes. Our Savior has compassion on us in our sorrows. When your emotions are unstable, if you're wounded, betrayed or rejected, know that He feels your pain. He will give you an overflow of grace and mercy to help you when you need it most.

Your Cups Running Over

In Psalms 23, the cup overflows with blessing, yet there are different types cups throughout scripture. We all know that cups are containers that hold contents for drinking or carrying something. Jesus is touched by our infirmities because instead of the cup of blessing, He was willing to ingest the cup of suffering.

"Then Jesus went with them to the olive grove called Gethsemane, and he said, "Sit here while I go over there to pray." He took Peter and Zebedee's two sons, James and John, and he became anguished and distressed. He told

them, "My soul is crushed with grief to the point of death. Stay here and keep watch with me. He went on a little farther and bowed with his face to the ground, praying, "My Father! If it is possible, let this cup of suffering be taken away from me. Yet I want your will to be done, not mine." Then he returned to the disciples and found them asleep. He said to Peter, "Couldn't you watch with me even one hour? Keep watch and pray, so that you will not give in to temptation. For the spirit is willing, but the body is weak!" Then Jesus left them a second time and prayed, "My Father! If this cup cannot be taken away unless I drink it, your will be done."
Matthew 26:36–42 (NLT)

This cup of suffering would represent the judgment from the sin of the world poured out on Jesus. This cup of suffering would bring about a new covenant of grace. Jesus took into Himself what He didn't earn and didn't deserve so that we may have what we don't deserve and couldn't earn. Mercy and grace in our time of need.

As Jesus prayed in the Garden of Gethsemane, in the olive grove, He says, "My soul is crushed with grief to the point of death." Doesn't this statement portray what it feels like in the valley of the shadow of death? He is entering into what He called "the hour of His death." It was the purpose of His life to die for the sin of those who couldn't save themselves.

In verse thirty-nine (39), Jesus called that moment of crucifixion, "the cup of suffering." In the Greek, Jesus said to the Father, I'll do what You want. I'll face this bitter ordeal because Father, You've ordained it. I will go to the cross and ingest the contents of judgment for the sin of the world. Why? So all who believe on Him can have life more abundantly. Another way to say it, "cups running over!"

His cup of suffering was fully ingested. This is significant to note; you and I have been saved from God's wrath because Jesus had taken it all in. To those who believe on Jesus, there is no condemnation. We are free and free indeed. You and I can feast on the love of God and dwell in the house of The Lord forever!

This is important because perfect love casts out all fear. There's no reason to shy away from God because He's not out to get us or teach us lessons through harming His children. God's not in Heaven trying to kill, steal from and destroy His own children. He's giving mercy and grace to help us in our time of need.

He took the cup of suffering so that we can take the cup of salvation.

> *"I will lift up the cup of salvation and*
> *praise the Lord's name for saving me."*
> *Psalm 116:13 (NLT)*

Jesus relates to our bitter ordeals because He's literally been through Hell and back. Scripture teaches us that as He prayed in the place of crushing called Gethsemane, drops of blood came from His head. It's a condition called Hematidrosis, where blood comes out of the skin like sweat. That was the result of the physical agony and stress of carrying the weight of the sin of the world and of separation from the Father on the cross. This was a bitter cup.

The Father forsook him, so we'd never be alone. He was wounded for us so by His stripes we'd be healed. He was beaten and bruised in exchange for peace. Don't allow the adversary to steal your praise when you try to escape the pain. No matter what you're facing lift up the cup of salvation and praise the Lord for saving you. Instead of panicking under pressure, we should praise through the pain. We should do as Jesus did in the olive grove, fall on our faces and pray. Instead of sleeping through life without a clue to the times and seasons, wake up and pray with Jesus. Get up and seek God in the garden.

The disciples slept over and over again ignoring the invitation to pray in the moment of crushing, because they sought physical comfort more. There's nothing wrong with sleep, but there was another kind of rest needed for this kind of darkness. Let it not be said that you and I sleep at the hour of prayer. Instead, awake to fall on your face before God and get the grace to help in your time of need. Your prayer won't go unanswered. Heaven will take notice of your petition.

We've discussed cups, but for a moment can we talk about a bowl? It's filled with incense that sits in Heaven before God's throne. In the book of Revelation or the book of unveiling we see the powerful connection of our prayers in Heaven.

"Then I saw a Lamb that looked as if it had been slaughtered, but it was now standing between the throne and the four living beings and among the twenty-four elders. He had seven horns and seven eyes, which represent the sevenfold Spirit* of God that is sent out into every part of the earth.

He stepped forward and took the scroll from the right hand of the one sitting on the throne.

And when he took the scroll, the four living beings and the twenty-four elders fell down before the Lamb. Each one had a harp, and they held gold bowls filled with incense, which are the prayers of God's people."

Revelation 5:6–8 (NLT)

The Lamb is Jesus who was crucified. Now, He's alive and standing before the throne. When Jesus rose from the dead, Thomas the disciple was able to place his hands in the wounds from Jesus' crucifixion. In verse six (6), the Lamb looked as if it had been slaughtered, but this is the same Jesus who died and is now standing. He's alive! The suffering He endured then, He stands triumphant now. The test of death was temporary, but his testimony of life is forever.

Verse eight (8) speaks of twenty-four (24) elders in Heaven falling down before Jesus with harps and gold bowls. These bowls are filled with incense that the Bible calls the prayers of God's people. What an image of the impact and importance of prayers! As you cry out to God in faith according to His word, it rises to Heaven like incense. These prayers from God's saints, His people, accumulate in containers.

Your cup of suffering should lead to prayers of faith that fill the bowls of Heaven. For instance, in Luke 1:10, it was during the hour of incense that people began to pray and God's angel spoke to Zacharias. Could our greatest times of testing's lead to our greatest prayers of faith? Will these hours of affliction fill the bowls until they tip over and cause Heaven to run over on earth?

"...So don't you think God will surely give justice to his chosen people who cry out to him day and night? Will he keep putting them off? 8 I tell you, he will grant justice to them quickly! But when the Son of Man* returns, how many will he find on the earth who have faith?"
Luke 18:7–8 (NLT)

I still believe God is looking for people to have faith in this fallen world. No matter how bad it gets, we can be like Job, we will continue to trust God. Even if we don't understand the full scope of His plan, we trust that He knows what's best. The answer may not happen in our lifetime, but we believe He's able to deliver His people.

As believers we may fail to see the bigger picture through the struggle; the eternal perspective of His plan. Still, we must hope against hopelessness. Through all the ills of this world and the injustices throughout our history, God is just! Vengeance is His and He will repay. Those who have cried throughout their seasons of suffering in generations past will enter into God's rest. Every tear wiped from their eyes, they'll rest from their labors forever. The Lamb of God will see to it! God The Father will make all things new and restore His people.

It took me years to appreciate the Apostle Paul's aim in life. He told the people of Philippi:

"I want to know Christ and experience the mighty power that raised him from the dead. I want to suffer with him, sharing in his death, so that one way or another I will experience the resurrection from the dead!" Philippians 3:10–11 (NLT)

We can overcome suffering through the life of Christ within us. You and I can rise above the burdens within that weigh us down. Regardless of the physical reality of Death Valley around us, we will experience resurrection from the dead. With the same power that raised Jesus from death, we are able to overcome. Our cup runs over with the salvation of the Lord.

13. Faithing Through

> "Never be afraid to trust an unknown future to a known God."
> — Corrie ten Boom

The amount of faith we choose to place in our Heavenly Father depends on our perception of Him. The Bible is His revelation of Himself to us. It's the not the fullness of His deity, but it is enough for us to comprehend the purpose of faith. No mind can fully grasp the complexity of God. If I could "figure out" all there is to know about God, He wouldn't be God at all.

For our understanding He has provided us the foundation of our faith, the Bible. It is the inspired revelation of God given to us through the Holy Spirit.

"All Scripture is breathed out by God and profitable for teaching, for reproof, for correction, and for training in righteousness…"
2 Timothy 3:16 (ESV)

Within the pages of scripture we understand the characteristics or attributes of God's divine nature. There are many adjectives that could describe His personhood. I'd like for us to study three words to fortifying your faith: Omnipotent, omnipresent and omniscient. If we are to trust Him with our soul in this life and the life to come, we should get to know who The God of the Valley is.

Imagine with me for a moment that you could get a sample of God's DNA and put it under a microscope. (Obviously we can't do this so please bear with me.) You place the specimen under the lens to examine what He's made of and to see what flows throughout every part of His being. However, you wouldn't be able to miss these three attributes of His divinity through and through.

1. Trusting God's Omnipotence

God has unlimited power. Omnipotence is the reality of God's all-powerfulness. From Genesis to Revelations we bear witness to the might of God. He created the universe with the power of His words. What's more is there as His words went out to accomplish His will? He didn't loose virtue and His power never diminished.

> *"The Lord merely spoke, and the heavens were created. He breathed the word and all the stars were born."*
> *Psalm 33:6 (NLT)*

What a mighty God we serve! To Him there's no difference in creating the universe with a word and creating the wings of a bee. He owns all power all the time. He's everlasting and never runs out of strength. Do you remember the pink energizer bunny from the commercials? He keeps going and going. Eventually that bunny will burn out and he'll have to retire, but God won't.

Isaiah 40:28–29 (NLT)

28 "Have you never heard? Have you never understood? The Lord is the everlasting God, the Creator of all the earth. He never grows weak or weary. No one can measure the depths of his understanding. 29 He gives power to the weak and strength to the powerless."

There is no way for us to measure His understanding and power, but we experience the size of it when we look at salvation. When the power that raised Jesus from the dead enters your life, you witness a personal resurrection. Your sin is forgiven, guilt and shame are removed and the Holy Spirit fills you with His presence. This is real power, changing a sinner into a saint for all eternity while our lives are transformed by the working of God's power. He gives power to us in our weakness like electricity to a lightbulb. It enables the bulb to reach its full potential. We can trust in His ability to share His personal strength with us when we are weary.

God's power parted the Red Sea with Moses; it caused Mary to conceive Jesus and raised Lazarus from the dead. That same power conquered sin through the cross. It took the sting out of death and the victory out of the grave. His power will cast death and Hell away forever and it will bring about a new Heaven and a new Earth.

Now, with God's unlimited power comes great responsibility. He sovereignly exercises His power as He wills. He always has a plan and with every action He has a purpose. This is because His power flows in conjunction with His omniscience.

2. Understanding God's Omniscience

Our Creator is not only all-powerful, but He's also all-knowing. To say that God is intelligent or knowledgeable falls short of describing the enormity of

His abilities. There's no IQ test to measure the vastness of His understanding. He can't get any smarter and there's nothing new for Him to learn or discover. He's the beginning and the end of all things. He sits outside of the time He created and works within it from His omniscience while clearly aware of all that He is and all that is within creation. So when God uses His power, it is to His own glory and it is used to bring about His own will.

It would do us well to remember that this life isn't all about us. Our lives are part of a greater narrative, the story of God. It's a blessing to be included in history or His story.

Nothing escapes the scope of God's knowledge. Throughout all creation not one detail was hidden from Him.

Psalm 50:11 (NLT):
"I know every bird on the mountains, and all the animals of the field are mine."

Isaiah 40:26–27 (NLT):

26 "Look up into the heavens. Who created all the stars? He brings them out like an army, one after another, calling each by its name. Because of his great power and incomparable strength, not a single one is missing. 27 O Jacob, how can you say the Lord does not see your troubles? O Israel, how can you say God ignores your rights?"

Throughout the universe there's nothing new to God. He knows every comet and galaxy by name. Even the hairs on our body have a number assigned to them in the mind of God. Isaiah speaks to the concerns of the people in verse twenty-seven (27). God's omniscience enables Him to see every detail of our troubles. We must trust that He will not ignore our rights. In other words, God will use His power and wisdom to make right all the wrongs against His children and He will bring justice for the innocent. We may not understand how and we don't know when, but He will.

Jesus alludes to the all-knowingness of The Father with His capacity for detail and His love for His creation.

Matthew 10:29–31 (NLT):

29 "What is the price of two sparrows--one copper coin? But not a single sparrow can fall to the ground without your Father knowing it. 30 And the very hairs on your head are all numbered. 31 So don't be afraid; you are more valuable to God than a whole flock of sparrows."

We shouldn't worry about our lives for our future, our hopes and our dreams are safe in the hands of God. When we face situations that seem unfair lean not to your own understanding but acknowledge Him. Faith your way through the doubts and trust Him.

The sparrows are lesser beings than humans. Back in the days when they were sold in the marketplace, their value was minimal at best. That didn't stop God from keeping a watchful eye over each of them. Jesus then opens our eyes to the way God thinks about us. Since we are more important than the birds to Him, He watches over us at all times. There's never a time to be afraid of our lives for God is all-powerful, all-knowing and He's there for us no matter where we are.

3. He's Omnipresent

God is present everywhere at the same time. Talk about having a super power! The Bible describes Him as sitting on a throne in Heaven. This is a reality but God is also everywhere at the same time. The Apostle Paul wrote of the preeminence of Christ. That is the superiority of Christ. What you'll find in this passage of scripture are connections of God's divine attributes.

Colossians 1:16–17 (ESV)
16 "For by him all things were created, in heaven and on earth, visible and invisible, whether thrones or dominions or rulers or authorities--all things were created through him and for him. 17 And he is before all things, and in him all things hold together."

By Him all things come to be. That's God's omnipotence. Everything came through and for Him. That's His omniscience at work. Not only does He know all the details about these things, but also, He has the knowledge to bring them to fruition. He also has a sovereign agenda at work here as well. Yet, He holds all things together in Himself. That's His omnipresence. Let's see these attributes at work together again within the Bible narrative.

Acts 17:24–28 (NLT)

24 "He is the God who made the world and everything in it. Since he is Lord of heaven and earth, he doesn't live in man-made temples, 25 and human hands can't serve his needs-- for he has no needs. He himself gives life and breath to everything, and he satisfies every need. 26 From one man he created all the nations throughout the whole earth. He decided beforehand when they should rise and fall, and he determined their boundaries. 27 "His purpose was for the nations to seek after God and perhaps feel their way toward him and find him--though he is not far from any one of us.

28 For in him we live and move and exist. As some of your own poets have said, 'We are his offspring.'"

You see God's sovereignty in creation. Omnipresence: He's not limited to man-made temples as His abode. He has no needs because He never lacks strength or understanding. He knows the plan for every kingdom and human being in the world before they ever came into existence.

Verse twenty-eight (28) tells us that in Him we live and move and exist. There's no valley that we walk through where we disconnect from God and we are never out of the reach of His care. There's never a problem so great that has taken God by surprise. You're never so far in trouble that you've left the confines of His concern. You can place your faith Him no matter where you are or what you're facing.

Throughout the Psalms, God is called our refuge, a hiding place for us in the time of trouble. He's our shelter from the harsh elements of life. You can find all that you need within Him. He's always there with an unlimited supply for every situation. One of my favorite verses is Psalm 46:1:

> "God is our refuge and strength, a very present help in trouble." Psalm 46:1 (ESV):

Again, we see that He's filled with strength, He's present and He's intelligent enough to help us in our times of trouble so we have no need to fear the shadows of death. Jesus makes it more personal than what we've discussed. Not only is God ever-present around us, but He will live within us.

16 "And I will ask the Father, and he will give you another Advocate, who will never leave you. 17 He is the Holy Spirit, who leads into all truth. The world cannot receive him, because it isn't looking for him and doesn't recognize him. But you know him, because he lives with you now and later will be in you."
John 14:16–17 (NLT)

We have a friend in the Holy Spirit! He's available to comfort us through our mountain top moments and He's there for us in the lowest valley. We don't have to do life alone; you can faith your way through whatever life throws at you.

Great Misunderstandings

Our faith should be strengthened by these attributes but if our understanding of how they work together is incomplete, they may distress us. What I'm referring to here are those moments of doubt caused by our faith. I mean, if God is all-powerful, why doesn't he just remove cancer altogether? It's not too hard for Him to do right? The Bible says that He's all knowing, so why did He allow me to get laid off? He saw that coming lightyears away. Couldn't He have given me a heads up? Since He's everywhere at all times, why didn't He stop that natural disaster from taking so many lives? These are the doubts or questions that come to mind as a result of what seems to be a conflict with our faith. When things didn't turn out as we've prayed they would, what then is the issue? Is God omnipotent, omniscient and omnipresent or not?

> *"Faith is not the belief that God will do what you want. It is the belief that God will do what is right."*
> *Max Lucado, He Still Moves Stones*

He is in fact all that we've discussed, which is all the more reason for us to trust in His sovereignty rather than to trivialize His existence in light of suffering. We live in a world that has been in need of repair since the fall of man. One day God will make all things new. He gave us prophecy of a new Heaven and Earth to give us hope. Our confident expectation for everything we have seen and have experienced isn't all there is; God will have the final amen! He is the final say! He says that He will, in time, make all things new. He will bring justice and all will be right in this world.

Since He works all things after the counsel of His will we must trust that with His super powers, He has a super plan. I will not presume to know all the details within said plan because it's too much for us to fathom. Yet, this doesn't negate faith. In fact, it strengthens the need for us to believe beyond what we can know or see with the naked eye.

When we pray for a miracle in sincere faith and it doesn't happen as we'd hoped, He's still God. Sometimes things aren't fair in this fallen world. Its not about what we deserve or didn't earn.

Calamity happens to the best and worst of humanity. Our faith isn't a tool to wish away what we don't want, nor is faith in God the ability to get whatever we want whenever we want it. He never promised to do everything we desired for Him to do. That's a misunderstanding. If we send up our prayers through a warped perspective we are setup for disappointment.

Faith is our confidence in God to be who He is, sovereign with His power. Sovereign means that He can do what He wants when He wants within His perfect will. He's God. It's His story and in the end, we will understand the when's and why's of this life.

Every parent out there can relate to this; we know that our children can't have everything they want when they want it. We may exercise our right to grant some request, but then choose not to give other request. If we see that their desire is not in their best interest the request may be denied. Or sometimes what they want is a 'not yet.' Other times, it's a 'you're never going to get that under my roof!'

In our eyes, at the time we make certain request it seems like what is best. Especially when what we're requesting is relief from suffering, injustice or pain. And there's nothing wrong with requesting these things, but we must, in addition to that, trust God's timing. We must be confident that our heavenly Father loves us.

9 "You parents--if your children ask for a loaf of bread, do you give them a stone instead? 10 Or if they ask for a fish, do you give them a snake? Of course not! 11 So if you sinful people know how to give good gifts to your children, how much more will your heavenly Father give good gifts to those who ask him."
Matthew 7:9–11 (NLT)

Our Father will provide what we need. Sometimes we don't quite know what we need within our limited perspective and so what we ask for and what God supplies maybe different. Know this, He never ignores us because He only ever loved us. This is another of God's attributes that we must seek to understand and place our faith in.

He won't give us a snake in place of a fish. He's a good Father to His children. Now, as with my own children, they may interpret my 'not yet' for a 'no.' They may believe that my no is inconvenient. Though we differ in opinions and strategy, I love them and know what's best for them.

As my children have grown older, they've come to appreciate my ancient wisdom because I've proven to be right about some things. They've learned to trust me in moments where they don't understand. Why? Because I've walked through the jungles of life and come out on the other side. Why should they blaze a trail the hard way when I've already paid the price to get the wisdom? I've suffered bad choices to give them wise counsel for free. They should trust and follow my lead in life.

God has already seen the end from the beginning. He knows what's best because well, He's been there and done it and He knows the right way. We have to trust that He's already in our future and in a moment this will all make sense. I don't have to understand it but as long as He does, that is all that matters. Faith says, God I'm riding with You on this journey; Your Kingdom come and Your will be done.

We are not exempt from suffering in this life but we are guaranteed a relationship with God through it all. Faith your way through valleys of confusion. Those moments where your beliefs get rocked to the core by the horror of what has taken place in this world. There are heinous acts of terrorism that jolt our souls, but that's not the time to pull away from the Father. It's the time to draw near to Him no matter what it seems.

He's proven that in sending His only begotten Son to die for us, He redeemed us all. He's now patiently giving people in this world time to repent. This is a time of grace that allows the gospel to be preached throughout the whole world and at the right time, the period of grace will end setting in motion the tribulation and the final end. For eternity things will be made right and all the sufferings of our present time will pale in comparison to the glory that will be revealed!

Until then, our souls are in the hands of our all-powerful, omniscient, omnipresent and loving God. Continue to listen to the Holy Spirit and become persistent in pursuing God's presence. Knowing that no matter what happens in this world you have eternal life with the Father. This body will die but your spirit will live on forever with God. Soak in the words of Jesus our Savior for a moment.

27 "My sheep listen to my voice; I know them, and they follow me. 28 I give them eternal life, and they will never perish. No one can snatch them away from me, 29 for my Father has given them to me, and he is more powerful than anyone else. No one can snatch them from the Father's hand."
John 10:27–29 (NLT)

You are in the hands of The Father! He's more powerful than anyone or anything else. God is more powerful than disease, addictions or abandonment. God is holding you right now in the palm of His hands if you're His child. Whatever accesses us in the physical realm, must be allowed through the grip of His fingers. Nothing can touch us without passing through His firm grip around our lives first.

Jesus pointed to something powerful in verse twenty-eight (28). Jesus gives eternal life, translation: we never die in His eyes. He's saying that no matter what happens in our physical bodies in this lifetime, we live on. Your worst enemies on this earth are sin and death. Jesus defeated both through the finished work of the cross and now that our greatest enemies are gone, we will and have overcome this world through our faith.

The greatest victory for a believer is not a material breakthrough. It is the eternal life of Jesus that broke through the death that was in our hearts. We are alive in Christ Jesus. Don't miss this point beloved.

God blesses His people with prosperity, physical healings and possessions of all kinds, but none of those things will carry on into the next life. You can't take your car, house or money to heaven with you. These monetary blessings are also momentary. God and you are eternal and your relationship with the God of the valley is greater than any blessing He could give you.

Don't misunderstand God's silence in our moments of shouting. We're upset because He hasn't responded in the manner we've requested within an allotted time we've set for Him. Be careful not to allow our hearts in our disdain to pronounce false accusations against our Father saying He doesn't or didn't love us as much as the Bible claimed.

Gaining an Eternal Perspective

In our short sightedness we miss God's bigger, eternal plan. Please understand that I still believe God provides miraculous provisions in this material world, but He invites us to explore a deeper level of blessing. The blessings of an abundant life from the supernatural realm.

We must be careful that we don't fall into the trap of making God The Sovereign our Santa Clause. There's more to the believer's walk of faith than God granting our every wish. In fact, it's faith through the darkness that shows the world our relationship with the invisible God.

Consider the Apostles and early church fathers. Most of them were killed for advancing the gospel; some were crucified upside down, stoned to death and or imprisoned. What if their relationship with Jesus was predicated on fairness? What if their commitment to Christ was contingent on their comfort? I'm sure they would've quit because it wouldn't have been worth it to stay the course. These were men and women of faith. They maintained an eternal perspective through their sufferings. Take for instance the Apostle Paul. He's writing in his letter to the Church at Corinth about what he'd endured for the sake sharing eternal life. Go with me to *2 Corinthians 4:8–18 (NLT),* and read with me these few verses of scripture.

Paul has an eternal perspective! This is why their preaching increased while their suffering increased. They couldn't suppress their faith and they did not give up! While going through questionable circumstances they didn't even question God. Paul said, "Their bodies were dying, but something was taking place within them. Their spirits were renewed daily."

It's as if an awareness of the life to come was fresh within them. They accepted the reality of the cruelty in this life but they knew the gospel was the way to reshape evil in this world. God's coming Kingdom was the solution for this world and they shared this message relentlessly.

For in their minds this world as they knew it would cease, but the lives changed with the gospel would live eternally.

One day, the various things that plagued us in this life will be gone. Our present struggles won't last forever and if you look at it in the grand scheme of things, they're actually quite small. There's a glory that's to come too. When God makes all things new, it will be a glorious day when the Father rewards the faithful, those who've endured till the end.

Look to that moment. Fix your eyes on the realm that you cannot see. Slip into the eternal while in the present and you'll understand that all the troubles you've overcome will be worth it. So don't loose heart. Don't give up on God. Stay the course and faith through it. For the God of the Valley is walking with you.

At your greatest point of suffering, in your greatest time of need; by your side you will find Him and forever He will be...The God of the Valley.

~Sean Reed

www.ingramcontent.com/pod-product-compliance
Lightning Source LLC
Chambersburg PA
CBHW021006110526
R18275700001B/R182757PG44588CBX00010B/17